Beyond Patriarchy

Beyond Patriarchy

WOMEN AND MEN IN THE EVOLUTION OF A POST-PATRIARCHAL WORLD

PATRICIA KRAUS, PH.D.

ISBN-13: 978-1500303419
ISBN-10: 1500303410

For my daughter
Julianne

Acknowledgments

For many years my daughter Julianne and I lived in a household that was predominantly male even to the sex of our dogs. I am very grateful for her as my gender companion. But I am also grateful for the testosterone environment as well, because it afforded me the opportunity to observe the development of the male psyche. I became a stronger more disciplined woman. So I thank my husband Ted and my sons Michael, Martin, Richard and Daniel for the overall evolutionary opportunity they provided for me. In addition, I am grateful to George Schaeffer, Ferde Hirtler, Brian Turkington and Gene Thomas who are all deceased, as well as Eddie Mudrak, John Hughes and Greg Kay all still living. All of these gentlemen allowed me a deep insight into the adult male/female relationship. We could discuss absolutely anything. Greg steered me onto the discussion of the evolutionary path as the crucial central topic for this book. I also want to acknowledge Agnes Barba, Peggy Klanica and Cathleen Murtha who read the manuscript and gave feedback regarding what it meant to them. Gratitude is owed to my editor Stephen Spignesi and my agent John White.

Contents

Introduction

I could not have written this book ten years ago, even though I wanted to write for at least five years prior to that. I had plenty of data but could not focus on how and where to begin. Even though I continued to do literature searches, I was not able to focus. I explored astrophysics, geology, archeology, cosmology, psychology, sociology, religion, theology and economics in order to define the story.

This activity only broadened the picture more and more and left me feeling more confused.

When I finally met my editor, he guided me in the direction in which I needed to move. Also, a close friend suggested I take an *evolutionary* approach to the "story" I wanted to tell. Between the suggestions of these two men I was set to go. Once I started to write, the story took its own path and pace. That seemed to me to be the way many authors found themselves guided. The direction developed on its own as if it came from somewhere beyond me. Taking the evolutionary approach proved to be stimulating and exciting, and allowed a significant broadening for my own research.

As I worked on a chapter I could already visualize where the next one would lead, a rather amazing awareness for me. It was as if my own evolution was further involved. I decided to write the evolutionary drama in three distinct parts, expecting each chapter in a part to build on the previous ones. Still, at times I seemed to be in a quandary, knowing what I wanted to include in the following chapters, but needing to give myself more time to clarify it.

In part one I decided to discuss the universal evolutionary trajectory as it is described by science and interpreted by cosmologists and developmental psychologists. The difficulty that many people have with the evolutionary story is directly related to what is known as *dualistic* thinking—either *or* descriptions. For me, the concept of evolution requires *unitive* thinking. Though God is changeless, the divine presence inherent in the universe is continually changing it in a variety of ways. This inner Wisdom knows what it should do.

Chapter one describes the general scientific view of the universe from the point of the "Big Bang" up to the emergence of mammals. Chapter two looks at the emergence of primates and hominoids, and traces the evolution of humanity through at least 3,000,000 years up to the present day. In chapter three I discuss several approaches to understanding the evolution of humanity, from theorists of various disciplines, going beyond mere Darwinian perspectives. Chapter four provides a description of the effect that human consciousness has upon the evolutionary process. Because evolution *denies* that humankind stands apart from nature and the natural processes that shaped the rest of the living world, humans are now in the position of *consciously* needing to choose how to take care of our planetary environment as well as our species. Thus, humanity has become responsible for whether or not we continue to evolve or continue to destroy ourselves and our planet. Chapter five describes the evolutionary adult development for both men and women, which is necessary for the personal, cultural and collective healing of humanity.

In part two I present evidence regarding many of the changes occurring in society today—the new evolutionary journey that has emerged and continues to pressure humanity in a positive direction despite what appears to be a regression. We are simply more conscious of what has been occurring for a century or more. Chapter six describes how women are finding their own *voices* and breaking free from the co-dependency with males, that has existed for thousands of years. Chapter seven looks at the actual role women are beginning to exert globally as a result of finding their own voices. The emergence of women in many aspects of society worldwide is having very positive effects while simultaneously shaking up the cultures that have existed for so long. Chapter eight inquires about the chaos that is occurring due to the breakdown of male control—the patriarchal system—and the difficulties we experience as a result. This breakdown is affecting every aspect of our experience globally today. We are all in this together, for good or for ill.

In part three the topics refer to where we go from here. Chapter nine describes the need for a *spiritual evolution,* one that goes beyond ego and individualism to a recognition that we belong to the universe and must be responsive to it. We must become *transpersonal,* plumbing the depths of our innate, hidden, evolutionary Wisdom. Several models of spirituality present a multifaceted picture of what we need to do to evolve as the human race. The wisdom to accomplish this is already imbedded in the human psyche just waiting to be discovered and initiated by each person. In chapter ten I emphasize the necessity of developing a *contemplative attitude* toward our personal experience as well as toward the crises in the world today. Becoming aware of the chaos that is pushing us to an entirely new strategy for world peace and intergenerational healing requires an understanding of forgiveness for which I provide empirical evidence. I also provide several accounts of men and women who have changed their worldview because of a contemplative attitude toward their life experience.

By taking this approach to human development, via universal and planetary evolution as well as the rise of consciousness, I hope to show that we are all connected to each other, and everything else, within an *ever-changing* Divine Plan. In spite of this ongoing change, the Plan was set from the beginning and moves ever forward to fulfill its destiny guided by its inherent Wisdom.

PART ONE
the Drama of Evolution

CHAPTER ONE
Broadening the Concept of Evolution

Theory and Evidence

Evolution began with the "Big Bang." As science now understands it, the universe emerged as energy which exploded and produced hot, dense plasma some 14 billion years ago. The plasma slowly unfolded into galaxies and stars to produce planets in some of these star systems, creating what we call space. Some of those planets gradually brought forth life and, eventually, one of them allowed the appearance of human beings on earth.

There are three basic creation and evolution theories. The first is held by evangelical Christians who believe in the inerrancy of the Bible and strictly adhere to the creation stories, Genesis 1 and 2. It is referred to as "creationism." For them, creation was a six-day event. This view has been effectively and irrefutably debunked scientifically, largely because science now understands the immense span of time needed to produce the universe as we have come to know it, and that the order which Genesis describes as the succession of creative emergence does not fit the evolutionary picture. In this view "creation" can not be evolution.

A second view is the Darwinian evolutionary perspective. This posits that the universe emerged randomly, even in regard to life, and that only the "fittest" survive. This concept of randomness takes into account environmental interventions that include weather patterns and natural disasters. The chief difficulty with this view is that no one who holds this view *strictly* has been able to credibly explain how, where and when the Big Bang occurred. Where did it come from?

The third approach, which has only recently been openly discussed, is known as "intelligent design." Many evangelicals want to include this in their school science programs along with teaching evolution. However, though this theory asserts God as creator, it has been discouraged by educators because it is viewed as a religious approach, and the scientific community sees it as antithetical to the study of science. At the heart of this is the controversy regarding the separation of church and state, as well as the fact that intelligent design is considered to be a refinement of "creationism."

My own perspective is that there is no discrepancy between a belief in God and Darwinian evolution. In spite of the fact that fundamentalist religions vehemently oppose a compromise with modern scientific thought, I agree with Swimme[1] who points out that "the opportunity of our time is to integrate science's understanding of the universe with more ancient intuitions concerning the meaning and destiny of the human." And Glynn[2] asserts that "advanced twentieth-century science is *closer in spirit* to the vision presented in the Book of Genesis than anything offered by science since Copernicus." This conclusion has been the result of the extension of the concept of evolution into theological realms, whereas it was once viewed so deeply opposed to faith.

As it turns out, the universe is not so random after all. It is now recognized that the ratios between the values of the fundamental forces of physics—gravity, electromagnetism, the nuclear strong force, and the nuclear weak force—are constants. If these constant values were even minutely other than we know them to be, a vastly different universe would have resulted. There is nothing random about the universe. And furthermore, many scientists now believe that "from the very beginning. . .the universe that we inhabit appears to be expressly designed for the emergence of human beings."[3] It seems that somehow the universe knew in advance what it was going to be in order to even begin. And because human beings are conscious that they are conscious, humanity has become the consciousness of the universe. We can now view the design of the universe much the way we understand software in a computer. It informs the universe how it should proceed in time. I prefer to call this *innate* design, or even "divine" wisdom.

Where and when does the idea of randomness enter the picture? Charles Darwin joined an expedition to circumnavigate the globe aboard the H.M.S. Beagle on December 27, 1831. During a prolonged stay in South America he witnessed the events and effects of volcanic eruptions, earthquakes and climate change. Somewhat later, he was especially intrigued by his observations of the flora and fauna on the Galapagos Islands, some 600 miles west of the South American coast. He noted the differences between the four species of mockingbirds found on various islands and discovered fourteen subspecies of Galapagos tortoises. Some of the tortoise species were obviously dependent upon the lush vegetation found on certain of the islands, a result of the adequate rainfall, for nourishing their growth. One island, Isabela, has six major volcanic cones, and five of the areas delineated by these cones are occupied by different tortoise subspecies, all of which are isolated from each other by extremely arid, barren and rugged lava flows.

Darwin also observed fourteen species of finches which he considered a classic example of adaptation, the process by which one species gives rise to multiple species that occupy different habitats. There were tree finches, primarily insect eaters, and ground finches which feed mostly on seeds. Beak size was a reflection of the size of seeds or insects that were eaten. Darwin referred to this variation as natural selection.[4]

Peter and Rosemary Grant, a British husband and wife team of evolutionary biologists who have resided at Princeton University for some time, have visited the Galapagos Islands annually over a period of more than thirty years. They have noted that the populations of the various species of finches vary with climatic changes that alter plant and insect populations. When certain plant and insect populations change with rainfall variation, the bird populations do likewise. The Grants have concluded that their observations are proof of evolution and natural selection at work year after year.[5]

Our Planet Earth

Roughly 10 billion years after the Big Bang, between 4 and 5 billion years ago, our home planet formed from a collapsing cloud of gas in interstellar space at the same time as did the sun and the rest of our solar system. "Our form of life needs a star like the sun, which inevitably was the product of a galaxy which itself formed from fireball fluctuations in the expanding universe."[6] It slowly condensed into a molten mass which was moving in an orbit around our sun. We have no data how much time elapsed before its orbit became elliptical or when it was sufficiently cool enough to begin to support life. The elliptical orbit guaranteed that there would be seasonal cycles of weather change, necessary to boost the emergence of life. Not only was our planet orbiting the sun, it was also spinning on its own axis creating the phenomenon of day and night. All of this was due to the "programming" I refer to as innate wisdom. Our planet earth was following its own evolutionary path.

The elements already present in the molten mass began to form chemical compounds, preparing the planet for the beginning of life. Hydrogen and oxygen were joining to form water molecules, most probably as steam. Carbon was uniting with oxygen to produce carbon dioxide and with hydrogen to form methane. Of all the elements, carbon is the one absolutely necessary for life. There are no living organisms without molecules containing carbon. This is due to the unique atomic structure of carbon. Nitrogen, along with hydrogen, oxygen and carbon, was preparing to form amino acids, the building blocks of living organisms.

Living things are able to reproduce; they can make copies of themselves. The first life forms are thought to have formed in the oceans in a kind of "primeval soup" where the chemical compounds had reached the conditions necessary to initiate life. Evidence from the rocks of the earth's crust indicates bacteria and blue-green algae were present over 3 billion years ago, and only about 1.5 billion years after the earth cooled and solidified.[7] Today, all life on earth is built on the same replication mechanism, the life molecule, DNA.

Along the way, some of the single-celled organisms began to produce oxygen as a by-product of photosynthesis, much like plants. During photosynthesis, light energy from the sun is absorbed by sensitive molecules, and then used to initiate a series of chemical reactions which are beneficial to the entire organism. This original struggle of single-celled organisms for survival was very slow. However, the gradual buildup of oxygen in the atmosphere produced two important effects: the production of ozone, forming a protective shield over the earth which modified temperature, and the accumulation of oxygen gas, which accelerated the generation of oxygen breathing organisms. This process began to evolve around 1.5 billion years ago and apparently proceeded much more rapidly than the earlier development of single-celled organisms.

Single-celled organisms reproduce by splitting, a process known as asexual reproduction. Virtually everything else we see reproduces sexually, with two different types of "parent" required to produce the succeeding generation. A few exceptions can be found in plants which can reproduce sexually or asexually. Apparently when two organisms are involved in the reproductive process a greater variety of outcomes can occur due to the splitting of the DNA molecules from each parent and the recombining across the two parental contributions. Thus, sexual reproduction became the more successful form and contributed to a wide diversity of species.

From a strictly scientific standpoint, natural selection has been leading to the production of multi-cellular organisms and the diversification of species since the very beginning of the emergence of life. Some "older" forms of life which have continued to reproduce effectively have not been replaced and are still with us today. Gribben states that no organism really *wants* to evolve, and changes only happen by "mistake."[8] I do not agree. There is an obvious innate design or divine wisdom in operation since the very beginning of time.

The evolution of both plants and animals was aided by another form of evolution as well—the movement of large land bodies due to the shifting of tectonic plates on the earth's surface. This gradually separated some land masses and jammed others together forming mountain ranges. In either case, new animal and plant habitats were formed, which allowed new possibilities for biodiversity. There were also a number of ice ages which caused the extinction of some organisms and allowed new opportunities for the survival of others. This type of evolution, part of the innate design of the planet, in many cases was much more rapid and chaotic.

The Science of Chaos

In the mid-twentieth century, "chaos" became a subject of interest in many fields of study. Among them were the earth sciences: geology, paleontology, meteorology, animal extinctions, ice ages, and so forth. A fascination with this concept also occurred with chemists, biologists, astrophysicists, even economists, and stock and real estate brokers. More and more researchers felt the futility of studying parts in isolation from the whole. For them, chaos was the end of the reductionist program in science. Yet there was little agreement on the word itself. One researcher noted that if an area of study like chaos began to grow, "it has to be because some clump of people feel that there's something it offers them—that if they modify their research, the rewards could be very big."[9] Many became convinced that chaos was a newly recognized class of natural phenomena. Some perceived order in it, while others believed it to be completely random.

These scientists—whether physicist or biologist, mathematician or economist—gradually recognized chaos as a set of ideas which was shared by other scientists. They came to believe "that simple, deterministic systems could breed complexity; that systems too complex for traditional mathematics could obey simple laws; and that, whatever their particular field of study, their task was to understand complexity itself."[10] Thus, another aspect of evolution was recognized, one that was not random, even though it appeared to be, but somehow was part of the very nature of things.

Among geologists and paleontologists, a preoccupation with the effects of earthquakes, volcanic eruptions, and ice ages developed. Animal and human migrations and extinctions, and the appearance of new species claimed their curiosity. Among meteorologists questions arose regarding weather patterns involving hurricanes and tornadoes, and why and how these occur when they do. The study of the giant craters that have been left by meteorite collisions with the earth were investigated, and a belief arose that it was just such a collision that brought about the extinction of the dinosaurs some 65 million years ago. Such a catastrophe would have rendered the atmosphere unlivable for the large dinosaurs for a lengthy period of time, whereas smaller animals, which may have already evolved into birds and mammals, could find habitat in burrows and caves in order to survive. Today it is believed that the actual collision occurred at the tip of the Yucatan peninsula, in the area east of the Gulf of Mexico, creating an approximately 110 mi. diameter crater. It is not known if factors such as the release of volcanic gases, sulfur dioxide, and large amounts of air-born dust contributed to the extinction.[11]

There is evidence that even before the dinosaur extinction there was a massive extinction in the oceans. The evidence comes from researchers at the University of Chicago, paleontologists Lauren Sallan and Michael Coates, who studied ocean fossils. They discovered that from 360 million years ago, for a period of roughly 15 million years, there was relative *silence* in the fossil record, leading them to believe that the oceans were relatively barren. It appears that gradually other species evolved, perhaps already present but in the minority at the time of the overall extinction. These species were able to survive and most likely are the origin of much of the life-forms we recognize today.[12]

The Cosmologists

Science alone cannot adequately explain evolution, nor can the concept of intelligent design. We need the very ancient tradition of cosmology that may go back three hundred thousand years to the time when cave dwellers were haunted by the mysteries of the universe that filled them with both terror and delight.[13] Cosmology refers to the explorations of the origin, development, and destiny of the universe, "told with the aim of assisting humans in their task of identifying their roles within the great drama."[14]

It appears that the cosmological tradition may be inherent in the human psyche. In other words, cosmology represents an effect of the evolution of the human being. The importance of this tradition is its power to awaken deep convictions that lie in the innate design and wisdom of the human person.

Thomas Berry, cosmologist, ecologist, and theologian, spent his life studying in many fields, including astronomy, physics, biology, world religions, history and cultures, and biodiversity. Berry saw that the evolutionary process of the universe is fourfold: "first, the evolution of the galaxies and the elements; second, the evolution of the solar system and of the earth with its molecular and geological formations; third, the evolution of life in all its variety; and fourth, the evolution of consciousness and the cultural developments of the human order."[15] Thus, these four evolutionary periods form a continuous, innate, developmental pattern programmed over nearly 14 billion years from the time of the Big Bang.

Berry recognized that our scientific account of the universe "is the greatest religious, moral, and spiritual event" of the last few centuries.[16] But we humans do not yet acknowledge this. Our scientific venture "has been unable to understand the significance of its own achievements."[17] The emerging environmental and ecological fields show promise for attaining the understanding of how to take care of our planet and prevent further damage. We must develop a *spiritual* awareness of the meaning of our scientific achievements.

We are all familiar with the reaction of the astronauts on their first voyage to the moon, in 1969, when they were able to view and photograph the earth. They were filled with awe and wonder and described the earth in poetic, mystical, and spiritual language. Lovelock[18] regards the earth as a unified, living organism with an amazingly intricate capacity to grow, develop, and regenerate from its own *innate* resourcefulness. He refers to this as the Gaia hypothesis.

The "old cosmology" from centuries past, has been scientifically informed with ever new discoveries, which enable us to understand, in a new way, the universal forces that have existed from time immemorial. These universal forces, referred to as cosmogenesis, "describe the workings of the universe as one in a continuous state of becoming, begetting fresh life and possibility, ever changing and, thus, ever new. We can never fully comprehend what it is all about, and we don't need to, because an intelligent universe is capable of dealing with its own unfolding in an intelligent way."[19]

Summary

We have briefly traced evolution from the energy burst of the Big Bang, through the formation of galaxies and stars, to the birth of our solar system and our home planet earth. We described the emergence of life, the periods of chaos and extinction, and the various ways that mankind and science have interpreted all of this. Now we are challenged to unify our interpretations so as to better adjust to the reality of what we experience. How will we learn to live with the innate wisdom of the universe that surrounds us and of which we are a part?

In the next chapter we shall discuss the evolution of human beings—where, when, and how they emerged—and their continued development up until the present day. We shall see that the unfolding of the universe which produced humanity on the earth is now experiencing a reversal. The behavior of humans is now adversely affecting our planet.

CHAPTER TWO
The Evolution of Humanity

The Primates

Our species, *Homo sapiens,* belongs to the order of mammals known as "primates", which includes apes, monkeys, lemurs, baboons and several other smaller mammals including the tree shrew. It is believed that the earliest primates were nocturnal tree dwellers with forward-pointing eyes which provided binocular vision. The more than 60 million years of primate evolution have been marked by an increase in body size, a striking advance in intelligence, and the development of an increasingly complex social behavior.[20]

The monkeys evolved about 40 million years ago, followed by apes 10 million years later. Last of all came the hominids some time between 14 and 4 million years ago. The apes and hominids are collectively known as *hominoids.* Among the ape primates, the chimpanzee is the closest to humans, with its DNA more than 99.5 percent similar to ours. Gorillas and orangutans have slightly less DNA similarity.

Contrary to popular sociocultural belief, the implications of the evolutionary pattern indicate that apes are *not* the ancestors of humans. It is believed that the last common ancestor between all the hominoids was around 10 million years ago. The Asian apes (orangutan, gibbon, etc.) split off first; the African apes (chimpanzee and gorilla) branched off about 7 million years ago.[21] The evolutionary pattern resembles a tree, with branches extending out at various intervals and the central trunk moving upward leaving those branches behind. The earliest hominids also branched off and did not survive. As the best we can determine, *homo sapiens,* the species that we now recognize as our own, represents the uppermost branch of the tree. From my perspective, it is important to understand that this evolutionary pattern has been *innately* programmed into the developmental process that has produced *homo sapiens.* We shall discuss in a later chapter the ways in which it is still operative in evolution and human development today.

The Anthropologists in Africa

The difficulty that anthropologists encounter in finding and dating fossils, that relate to the *hominoids* in general, lies in the manner in which the species' remains were covered with earth deposits. In many cases the fossils were crushed so that it was very difficult to determine exactly what they represented. However, there is one method that shows significant promise, and that is potassium/argon dating. This method for dating *rocks* and *minerals* utilizes the rate in which radioactive argon gas is converted into potassium, allowing the capability of dating rocks as far back as 3 billion years ago.[22] The method analyzes layers of volcanic ash, which, during the heat and pressure of an eruption, have initiated an "atomic clock" from the potassium/argon conversion. Anything buried below that layer is older than that date and anything above is younger.[23] The earliest human-like species are dated at least seven million years old.

Pre-eminent among anthropologists who searched for hominid remains, are Louis and Mary Leakey and their son Richard. Louis was born in Africa, the son of Christian missionaries in Kenya. He originally intended to follow his father's footsteps as a missionary, but after an extensive education in England and a degree in anthropology, he decided to follow a fossil-hunting career instead and subsequently returned to Africa. This was in the year 1926 when Louis was in his early twenties.

His favorite exploratory site was the Olduvai Gorge in Kenya which had shown promise in earlier geological excavations. In 1931 Louis discovered well-worked handaxes, probably about a million years old, lying on a slope. By the mid-1960s Louis and his wife Mary had collected an impressive list of fossil finds from which some details of human history could at least be inferred. Today, Richard continues his work in Africa, along with other anthropologists, geologists, and archeologists.

The Evolutionary Pattern

Richard Leakey maintains that the development of anatomical and behavioral complexity in hominids over the evolutionary span of time suggests "that some kind of *guiding hand* is at work in the process of evolution, moving the course onward and upward to the ultimate pinnacle, the human species."[24] The higher *hominoids,* chimpanzees and gorillas, were vegetarians. The changes in dental structure and the adoption of an upright posture and gait seem to be the principle characteristics of the earliest hominids. It is now believed that changes in the manner that food was collected and processed by animals is the major factor in the development of upright behavior in hominids. This would also account for changes in the dental structure, now needed for grinding seeds and roots rather than *merely* the tearing of animal carcasses common to other animals. Human evolution probably took place in two ways: first, as a gradual modification, though the fossil record, in general, does not support this. Second, the fossil record of human evolution, though it does not rule out gradual change, seems to indicate that new grades of human ancestors *suddenly* appeared in the record. The origin of a new species always took place in a small group of individuals that were geographically isolated from the main population. The new species arose there and later took over the territory of the main species. Cataclysmic changes from earthquakes and volcanic eruptions, as well as the gradual movement of the earth's crust over millions of years provided opportunities for the isolation of small migrating groups. This type of change in human characteristics is evident still today in many parts of the world.

Yet the fossil records indicate that in a number of locations two or more species coexisted. It is the dental findings which suggest that one group was vegetarian, while another supplemented the diet perhaps with lizards, eggs, and even small mammals. A third group developed a diet in which meat became a significant food item. The Harvard paleobiologist, Stephen J. Gould[25], has maintained a modern biologically based view, that "*homo sapiens* is not the foreordained product of a ladder that was reaching toward our exalted estate from the start. We are merely the surviving branch of a once luxuriant bush." Gould did not believe that either natural selection or gradual evolution could account sufficiently for the changes in human characteristics. While it is generally accepted that mankind first evolved in Africa, evidence indicates that migration of these early species into Europe and Asia offered the opportunity for slightly different subspecies of *homo sapiens* to develop in Europe and Asia. An especially interesting example of coexistence is the discovery of a series of hominoids found in a number of sites throughout Europe. The cave dwellers were discovered in the nineteenth century in Germany, France and other sites. Over a period from about 1.5 million years ago to about 300,000 years ago, *homo erectus,* most probably having migrated from Africa, existed in Europe as a relatively stable species. It is believed that *homo erectus* is the rootstock from which modern humans evolved. Neanderthal man first emerged in the fossil record some 100,000 years ago, in Europe and the Near East, during a warm interglacial phase. Fossils have been found that seem to indicate intermediate forms between *homo erectus* and the Neanderthals. Nevertheless, skeletal remains of the Neanderthals, referred to as *homo sapiens neanderthalensis,* do not truly resemble modern man. They were too apelike, especially in regard to skull structure and the curvature of some of the limbs.

Though the arrival of the Neanderthals was relatively gradual, their disappearance appears to have been rapid. Another ice age had covered Europe and Asia and began to melt between 50,000 and 30,000 years ago. In the Near East the Neanderthals vanished during this period, about 40,000 years ago, while in western Europe they are found coexisting with Cro-Magnon man who appeared around 35,000 years ago. Cro-Magnon man is considered one of the oldest representatives of *homo sapiens sapiens,* the name by which modern man is known today. Though the Neanderthals are thought to have evolved from *homo erectus* in Europe, it is not clear whether they then gave rise to *homo sapiens sapiens.* Rather, they may have become an evolutionary dead end, while modern humans evolved directly from *homo erectus* independently of the Neanderthals.[26] We do not know even though evolution continued.

As the glaciers melted, grasslands appeared which supported large herds of bison, horse and cattle. Between 20,000 and 15,000 years ago the grasslands gave rise to thick forests so that the herds began to move eastward. Since the early humans were hunter gatherers, many followed the herds. Those tribes which stayed behind made their homes in the caves of the fertile river valleys of southern France and similar areas. This was the time of the Paleolithic era, when the walls of caves were painted and statues of goddesses were first carved.[27]

It is now believed that human *progress* really began during this inter-glacial period when humans were migrating to other areas. In the process of migration tribes met other tribes, began to barter and exchange ideas with each other, and initiated an era of *invention*. Scientists have begun to refer to this as *collective intelligence,* "the notion that what determines the inventiveness and rate of cultural change of a population is the amount of interaction between individuals."[28]

Early Religion and Goddess Worship

The goddess images, carved in stone, bone, and ivory, (and later in clay, copper, and gold) appeared across a vast expanse of land stretching from the Pyrenees to Siberia. Looking back at these earliest artifacts, we recognize that at a time when humanity experienced themselves embedded in Nature as part of the whole, their first image of life was the Mother. This ancient cosmology gave way later to a more complex tradition of worship of the Mother Goddess. Images of giving birth, of large breasts and enlarged abdomens occurred again and again, through the Neolithic era 10,000 years later, and on through the Bronze and Iron Ages.

Lithuanian archaeologist, Marija Gimbutas's work[29] has completely transformed our understanding of this important phase of human evolution. Gimbutas spent most of her adult life until her death studying the goddess figures of the Neolithic period, unearthing the treasures of the advanced civilization she had named 'Old Europe'. The area this encompassed includes Hungary, south and central Yugoslavia (Bosnia and Macedonia), Bulgaria, Romania, and eastern Austria. Earlier archaeologists had assumed the figures were merely fertility symbols, but Gimbutas' research, in which she discovered tombs and temples, led her to believe that the female artifacts represented Goddess worship.[30]

The settlements of Old Europe grew into villages and small towns housing several thousand people. These settlements existed for thousands of years before they occurred in western and northern Europe, most likely because of the development of agriculture. All kinds of skills were developed, including pottery, and stone and copper-working techniques, as well as a rudimentary linear script.

The evidence regarding these settlements was that they were matrilineal (the genealogical descent follows the female side of the family) or matricentric (a culture centering on the mother), but not necessarily matriarchal (a culture in which rule and power are held by women). The tools found there were those needed for creating various artifacts, for food preparation, and for the construction of shelters. There were no weapons uncovered in these settlements. All the archaeological evidence indicates that these cultures were egalitarian, probably democratic, and peaceful.

The Origin and Embeddeness of the Patriarchy

Another area that Gimbutas' studied in detail revolved around her investigation of the "Kurgan" culture. These Aryan Indo-Europeans were a "patrilineal, patrilocal, pastoral, and seminomadic group of peoples who, she believed, originated in the steppes of Russia. They were militaristic, produced weapons, and rode horses. Their religion centered upon male gods."[31] Agriculture was rudimentary, and their ceramic art poorly developed. They buried their dead in pit graves covered with an earthen mound rather than tombs as did the Old Europeans. Thus, the Kurgan culture was different in many significant ways from that of Old Europe.

A dominant patriarchal civilization began to arise in the Old European villages due to the invasions by the Kurgan peoples around 4,500 B.C.E. followed by two later invasions. The domestication of the horse, and the utilization of their military ability, gave the Indo-European invaders a strong advantage over the peaceful Old Europeans. Sometimes the people they invaded were assimilated and sometimes their civilizations were destroyed. But in every case the Kurgans imposed both their language and religion on the indigenous people. In the words of Marija Gimbutas, "The earliest European civilization was savagely destroyed by the patriarchal element, and it never recovered, but its legacy lingered in the substratum which nourished further European cultural development."[32]

The word "patriarchy" is relatively new in our modern vocabulary. When I use the word I do not think of it as a male thing, but rather, as a cultural system, which serves as an impediment to needed social change. In the past, this system probably worked to help the human race survive. But because we do not recognize our taken-for-granted assumptions regarding our culture, these assumptions become our "truth" which we are unable to challenge much less change. Thus, patriarchy has served to oppress women for millennia and ultimately to debase men. We shall consider several aspects of this problem in the next chapter.

But the real difficulty with patriarchy is that it represents more than a social or political arrangement or cultural institution. It reaches far back into our ideas of existence, even into the moral, ritual, and belief commitments of religion. Control and "maleness" were conflated so that imperial controls over populations were carried out in the name of the divine, and rulers had divine status.[33] This absolute authority was *codified* in the early seventeenth century as "the divine right of kings."

This "divine right" mentality, however, was present throughout the 2,000 year history of the Hebrew people prior to the Christian era and continues in Christianity to this present day. Though the Egyptians, Canaanites, Sumerians, Babylonians, Greeks, and Romans maintained female deities, the male gods had reached ascendancy. These cultures, having also been invaded by the Indo-Europeans, were essentially patriarchal. With the exception of a very brief period in the worship of the Egyptian culture, the Hebrews were the only people that worshipped a single male god. Monotheism later appeared in Christianity and finally in Islam.

The Patriarchal Legacy

The *male gods* of the period from 4,500 B.C. were warlike, punishing judges, whether they represented the monotheistic Hebrews, or the

Egyptians, Sumerians and others who also had female gods. Consequently, the males who worshipped these gods were likewise warlike and punishing in imitation. Berry[34] points out, that throughout Western history, we can identify four patriarchal establishments:

- the classical empires,
- the ecclesiastical establishment,
- the nation-state,
- the modern corporation and banking system.

These are exclusively male dominated and their primary fulfillment lies in terms envisaged by men. These establishments have maintained the patriarchal system up until the present day.

The Classical Empires

The classical empires first appeared in Egypt, where the ruler was revered as a god, and in Sumeria, where the ruler was a representative of the divine. These empires continued through the Assyrian and Babylonian rulers, through the Persian empire, and later into Greece and Rome. The many achievements of these empires were often the product of enforced slavery. Similar societies were found in Asia, in China and India. Wars were fought between these empires and the victors occupied the lands of the vanquished.

In the West, the succession of empire followed through the Byzantine and Holy Roman empires. Later on, the Dutch, Portuguese, Spanish, and British created empires overseas. In the meantime, Russia expanded her influence throughout the Eurasian continent. In the near East, the rise of Islam saw conflict that extended well into Africa and Europe. Many of these empires established their power through religious coronation ceremonies, granting divine status to imperial control. In these empires all the men ruled in terms of patriarchal norms of conquest.

In the *sacred writings* of the Hebrew bible we find a warring deity and warrior ideals. The Hebrews believed their God wanted them to vanquish other tribes, especially those that believed in the goddess. Though a more peaceful teaching arose in the gospels, it did not survive the challenge of later centuries when conflict became the way of survival.

The Ecclesiastical Establishment

The Western ecclesiastical establishment had an even greater impact than the political empire. Enclosed within the same cultural boundaries as the empire, but with greater intellectual and spiritual impact, as well as religious and moral authority, it had more profound consequences. Furthermore, the empire and ecclesiastical establishments struggled against each other, with the church maintaining the upper hand for more than a thousand years. The belief structures presented by the church, stemming from the Bible and tradition, were the chief determinants of the reality and values of Western civilization.

From the beginning of the Bible, in the book of Genesis, the Earth Mother Goddess was abandoned in favor of a Heavenly Father God. The net result was that we gradually lost touch over the centuries with our embeddedness in the natural world. Even though the Psalms of the Hebrew bible contain extensive references to the praise and honor due to natural phenomena, the church became preoccupied with the supernatural. In addition, the Bible narrative presents woman as the instrument for the entrance of evil into the world. And over the years the whole concept of the feminine became diminished. Women were relegated to subordinate status in the church by the rulership of men, which was assumed to be divinely determined.

Because women were identified with seduction and moral evil, they were excluded for centuries even from participation in the official choir for church liturgies, except within the enclosure of their own convents. During this period it was believed that women were not even blood-related to their own children. They were simply empty vessels for the growth and development of the "male seed". It was assumed that normally a child would be born male, unless something had happened to alter the conception.

The Madonna became the greatest cultural image of the medieval period. Because the Virgin mitigated somewhat the patriarchal concept of woman, during the 16th century a certain element in the church rejected her image as a "pagan" intrusion of the goddess into the Christian world. The divine Virgin can be considered as an effort to bring into the culture at least some remnant of the ancient Earth-Mother Goddess.[35] In fact, many early shrines of the goddess were "baptized" and became shrines of the Virgin Mother. This is especially true of those shrines relegated to the veneration of the *Black Madonna*. There are hundreds of such shrines throughout Europe. The Virgin was thought to be so powerful that she even served as a protection against God himself.

The Nation-State

The third patriarchal establishment arose after the 15th century, when the feudal states of the medieval period began to transition to the monarchies and city states of the renaissance and the later period. At the same time, the growing power of the commercial classes demanded greater participation in the business of government. Religious and political allegiances, formerly given to the universal, ecclesiastical establishment, were now pledged to the separate states then dominating the European world. The merchant classes, new technologies, and a growing literacy shifted attention to the secular realm. Devotion to the fatherland and celebration of the anniversaries of national revolutions became revered traditions.

With the growth of worldwide exploration, European nations began to consider themselves the saviors of the peoples of the world. This became their sacred, historical mission, and thus began colonial expansion. And even slavery was brought into their enterprise. The nation-state might be considered the most powerful institution ever invented for organizing and controlling human societies. The concept of national sovereignty ought to be considered the supreme example of patriarchal, aggressive power, representing male values of conquest and sovereignty. A vain effort at national security led to the conscription of men for military purposes. The concept of total war came into being and involved all the resources of the nation. Conflicts or threats of conflict were driven by a distorted sense of the sacred—patriotism. And all of this was carried out by men, for the ideals of men.

Women were without power, functioning in the home, caring for children, and serving men. As women had greater access to education, and with more leisure time, they became more and more dissatisfied with their exclusion from public life. In the United States women were not given the right to vote until 1920, in Great Britain until 1928. But the imbalance between men and women was no longer acceptable to women. In time, the feminist movement became the pervasive influence in our society.[36]

The Modern Corporation

The fourth, destructive manifestation of patriarchy is the modern corporation. The corporation provides jobs, which allow employees to earn money, with which they can buy anything and everything. No longer does the cycle of nature sustain us; now we live in an industrial and consumption cycle. This industrial society is so erratic that it can no longer be relied on to provide jobs consistently for its citizens. Joblessness is one of the most unendurable indignities in our present industrial economy.[37]

At the present time, the co-dependence between the corporation, the banking system, and the government has exacerbated the situation into near chaos. Corporations lobby for control of government through contributions to candidates they hope will promote their agendas. Once elected these officials seek to appease the corporations. The success of the corporations through these endeavors affects their stock market value, which in turn impinges on the banking system. The single criterion for success becomes profit, in many cases leading to out and out greed.

Summary

In this chapter we have traced the evolution of humanity through at least 3,000,000 years up to the present day. We have noted the changes in physical structure and diet from the most primitive of peoples. The migration of these groups resulted in variations, now referred to as races, in different parts of the world. Some groups settled into agricultural societies in Old Europe, while in other areas nomadic, warring tribes developed. The clash between these groups brought about new societies which eventually evolved into what we now refer to as patriarchy.

The next chapter will serve to illuminate the evolution of consciousness, how it has served to enhance humanity as well as the way in which it has led to violence and human misery.

CHAPTER THREE
The Evolution of Self-Consciousness

For the last 4,000 years or more, the evolution of human consciousness has gradually added another dimension to the evolutionary
process. No longer is the innate wisdom, along with additional impetus
from the chaos of natural disasters, sufficient to promote natural selection
and human evolutionary development. Now human beings can consciously choose whether they are *willing to cooperate* with the evolutionary process
or not. We shall consider some of the theories proposed for explaining the
evolution of self-consciousness.

Another View of the Eden Story

Ken Wilber[38] speaks of creation as a *kenosis,* or self-emptying of the
Divine Spirit, without loss of itself or separation from itself in any way. The
divine energy spilled out into the Void and finally erupted nearly 15 billion
years ago in the Big Bang. Thus began the journey of this divine energy
back to the Divine Spirit as the innate wisdom of creation.

Billions of years later, around 2,000 B.C.E., something happened to
homo sapiens which eventually was recorded as an allegory about the Garden
of Eden. Humanity had lived in an idyllic state, immersed in nature much
like the animals. But a gradual emergence from this state brought about
an awakening of consciousness to pain and suffering. This "Fall from Eden"
awakened mankind to a world that was *already* mortal and finite, though they

had not known it. In fact, it was not truly a Fall at all, but an actual "rising up" from pre-personal consciousness to the personal ego and self-consciousness.

The story in Genesis 3 is a fascinating one. The fruit of the tree in the center of the Garden, the tree of the knowledge of good and evil, was forbidden for Adam and Eve to eat under pain of death. The story continues to reveal that Eve was "tempted" by the Serpent in that she saw the fruit was beautiful, good to eat, and would provide *wisdom* if she ate of it. Thus she took it, gave some to Adam, they ate it and "their eyes were opened." But the Serpent, who convinced them that they would be like god, knowing good from evil if they did eat, actually symbolized the Great Goddess and her Wisdom. The Serpent symbolized Wisdom for all the goddess-worshiping religions among the people surrounding the Hebrew people. Adam and Eve's action, therefore, was not an "original sin" at all, but an evolutionary quantum leap in consciousness which brought about the ability to choose right from wrong, or the reverse. Eve, which means *Mother of all the Living,* did not bring evil into the world; we have her to thank, not to blame, according to Wilber. Berry[39] asserts, "Patriarchy becomes the *original sin,* the primordial and all-encompassing evil through all the generations of Western society during these past five millennia." I agree with Berry. After all, Yahweh God says to Eve:

> "I will multiply your pains in childbearing,
> you shall give birth to your children in pain.
> Your yearning shall be for your husband,
> yet he will lord it over you."[40]

Wilber's view of the Eden story is essentially in agreement with the scientific record of evolution to date, even though science today finds that early humans had no resemblance to Adam and Eve of Genesis. Scripture scholars also agree that the biblical account is neither history nor anthropology. Yet, on the whole, the Eden story represents a consciousness that is a pre-personal immersion in nature.[41] Thus the story of the Fall allegorically describes a "Great Reversal", the emergence of ego consciousness, which occurred around the second millennium B.C.E.

The Hadza People

A recent study has brought attention to a hunter-gatherer group living in Tanzania.[42] Known as the Hadza, they grow no food, raise no livestock, and live without rules or calendars. They are nomadic, with no permanent shelter. They have maintained their foraging lifestyle in spite of long exposure to surrounding agricultural groups. The Hadza have a language but no form of writing. Today, only a handful of such groups—some in the Arctic, in Papua New Guinea, the Amazon, and a few groups in Africa—maintain a primarily hunter-gatherer existence.

The Hadza are of great interest to anthropologists because they are seen as an example of what life was like before the birth of agriculture 10,000 years ago. About a thousand Hadza live in their traditional homeland. Some have moved close to villages and have taken jobs as farmhands or tour guides, but one-quarter of their population remain true hunter-gatherers. The Hadza do not engage in warfare; rather, they are a friendly people. They have never lived densely enough to be seriously threatened by an outbreak of infectious disease. They seem to live on a continuous camping trip, almost entirely free of possessions with the exception of a cooking pot, a water container, and an axe, which they can wrap in a blanket and carry over a shoulder. During the rainy season the Hadza construct little domed shelters made of interwoven twigs and long grasses, which can be erected in as little as an hour.

Though gender roles are distinct, women do not live under forced subservience to men. They are unwilling to accept bullying and are frequently the ones who initiate a breakup with their partners. Women gather berries and baobab fruit and dig for tubers. Men collect honey and hunt. They will eat almost anything they can kill and will share it with the entire group.

The chief reason that the Hadza have been able to maintain their lifestyle for so long is that their homeland has never been an inviting place. With a briny soil, scarce fresh water, and intolerable insects, no one else wanted to live there. It is definitely not a Garden of Eden. In recent years migrating populations have moved into their area. Because they are not a combative people they have almost always moved away.

Now there is nowhere for them to retreat. The Hadza will soon be forced to move into the agricultural community and to domesticate plants and animals. Only time will tell what kind of lifestyle they will experience.

The Decline of the Goddess

Shlain[43] has proposed that the invention of writing was the beginning of the decline of the Goddess. Sometime in the distant past of human evolution, speech replaced gesture as the principal means of communication. The delicately balanced use of the feminine right side of the brain with that of the masculine left side was essential for speech. This balance was upset with the invention of writing. We now know that the three speech centers are present *only* in the left brain. A fundamental change in the way people understood their reality was introduced with the written word that further reinforced the use of the masculine left side of the brain.

Before there was writing there were pictures. Wall paintings in caves and stone pictographs or rock art (petroglyphs) appear wherever people have lived, and are the garbled record of preliterate people. They are virtually indecipherable. Mesopotamia and Egypt began to flourish around 3,000 B.C. and each of them developed a unique form of writing.

The Mesopotamians

The first Mesopotamians were Sumerians, a diverse group of communities living in the Fertile Crescent between the Tigris and Euphrates rivers, in what is now called Iraq. By gouging tiny wedge-shaped marks with sharp sticks in wet clay tablets they invented the first written language using *cuneiform* figures. At first these figures were primarily pictographic, but in time they became increasingly abstract, symbolizing an idea, a concept, an object, or an action. However, these figures were not arranged in any linear fashion. Rather, they were placed haphazardly upon the surface of the tablet. Scribes needed to rely heavily on pattern recognition, using all the symbols, to make sense of the messages. The *cuneiform* writings were used mainly to record trade transactions or items used in temple worship or sacrifice. Gradually, recognizing the importance of their innovation, the Sumerians established schools to teach it.

Some 500 years later the Sumerians were conquered by a northern group of people, the Akkadians, who spoke a different language. The Akkadians adapted the *cuneiform* writing to suit their language through the invention of symbols which represented syllables of speech. Thus, a single character began to represent both an *image* of a noun as well as a *sound* of a word. Within a century of their conquest of the Sumerians, *cuneiform* writing was expressing a *phonetic* language. Soon the Akkadians began to understand that meaning could be made more accessible if the figures were arranged linearly. In this way their writing became more and more a masculine left-brained function.[44]

Virtually all societies invent creation stories to explain the presence of the physical universe, the puzzle of human existence, and the reasons for death and evil. Though the Sumerians revered the Goddess, the conquering Akkadians did not. In fact, the creation myth conjured up by the Akkadian priests, *The Seven Tablets of Creation,* was shocking in its virulent misogyny. This myth replaced previous creation myths, and was celebrated annually long after the Akkadians had been conquered by the Assyrians and Babylonians who arose to power later. The myth proposed that the universe was created through the slaying of the Goddess by the male God Marduk. Pieces of her dismembered body became various features of the created world.

The worship of Marduk coincided with the lifetime of the Babylonian chieftain Hammurabi, who composed a code of law written in the *cuneiform* script. Thus the decline of the Goddess was paired with the ascendancy of written laws. Grammar and laws are unique to the left brain.[45] Consequently, patriarchy, the dominant theme of Hammurabi's Code, increased its influence in Mesopotamian history due to the extensive, thousand-fold promulgation of written documents.

The Egyptians

The Egyptians invented a writing system that was entirely different from *cuneiform*. They developed a pictorial script we call *hieroglyphs* around the same time as the Sumerian script evolved. Despite its complexity, this was a surprisingly expressive writing system. Though able to express most ideas, some concepts presented challenges to the *hieroglyphic* pictorial system. To resolve this problem the Egyptians invented twenty five additional characters to represent the consonants in their spoken language. This is the principle of the alphabet, allowing the reader to sound out a word concept. Even though the Egyptian scribes had developed a rudimentary alphabet, they used it sparingly.

The Egyptians perceived the snake as a beneficent, vital creature, intimately associated with female sexuality, wisdom, and life. So connected in the Egyptian psyche were beneficent serpents and goddesses that the hieroglyph for goddess was the same as that for serpent.[46] However, when literacy became more firmly established, several masculine-based creation myths gained popularity alongside the feminine-based ones. Even so, the gods and goddesses remained the mainstay of Egyptian religion for the first fifteen hundred years of their dynastic history.

Sometime between 1,700 and 1,550 B.C.E. significant changes occurred in the Egyptian culture with the arrival of the *Hyksos* from the East. They infiltrated the valley of the Nile and took control over the eastern part of the kingdom. Most historians identify them as northern semitic Canaanites who most probably knew *cuneiform*. These foreigners exposed the Egyptians to Mesopotamian ideas. Within little more than a hundred years the *Hyksos* were overcome and the Egyptians were once more in control with great military pharaohs who extended their influence far and wide throughout the Nile River Valley.

Dramatic changes were on the rise because of the tumultuous events. Not the least of these was a major change in the style of writing. Scribes increasingly used a *hieratic script,* which, relying on the principle of phonetic pronunciation, gradually supplanted *hieroglyphics.* The lands between the Egyptian and Mesopotamian empires became inhabited with people who developed scripts that were hybrids of *hieroglyphic* and *cuneiform* writing systems. Among these were Midianites, Phoenicians, Canaanites, Assyrians, and others.

The Israelites

Wandering throughout this territory was another group of people, nomadic herders referred to as Habiru. Many scholars believe that the Habiru were the precursors of the Hebrews, later known as Israelites. They were a motley collection of tribes who would have eventually been amalgamated into other civilizations had it not been for their desire to communicate with each other. Someone or some group devised a simplified method of writing—the alphabet.

The ease with which people could learn to use this alphabet revolutionized communication. Instead of over six hundred *cuneiform* characters, or six thousand *hieroglyphs,* the alphabet contained slightly more than 20 letters. The literate elite were no longer the sole users of the written language. Now the lower classes could also learn to write and read.

The Israelites' exodus from Egypt, under Moses, occurred around 1,300 B.C. During the period following, for some 500 years, the biblical stories, including the Mosaic Law, were handed down within an oral tradition. Once the alphabet was codified these histories, traditions, and laws were written on sacred scrolls. Furthermore, the scrolls were written in a linear fashion from right to left. This dramatic change in mindset, which utilized the masculine left side of the brain more often, was primarily responsible for *fostering* the system of patriarchy among the Israelites, according to Shlain.[47]

Finally, the relentless spread of the alphabet brought about the demise of the Goddess because the Israelites now had only one masculine God, and were forbidden to worship the Goddess. However, it is noteworthy that, during the period when the Hebrew scripture was being written, especially after the return from the seventy year Babylonian captivity, the biblical writers began to personalize Wisdom as divine feminine.[48] It seems that the Israelites brought back with them the knowledge of the Goddess once again as a result of their long exposure to the goddesses of the Babylonians.

The Evolution of Consciousness

Jaynes[49] asserts that "the succession of subjective states that we feel in introspection has a continuity that stretches all the way back through phylogenetic evolution and beyond into a fundamental property of interacting matter." In other words, consciousness is present in all of creation, at least potentially. This is why it cannot be accounted for by natural selection alone. Consciousness is innate. It is only in human beings that self-consciousness has truly become activated. Human beings are conscious that they are conscious, a recognition that a person can reflect on his or her inner state.

Wilber[50] refers to this innate potential as the *ground unconscious* from which all of nature has evolved. He also recognizes that natural selection is not sufficient to account for this emergence. Both Wilber and Jaynes agree with other writers that each human being lives out this emergence of consciousness in his or her life experience from conception, through birth, to death.

When Jaynes refers to the *bicameral mind* he is describing the functions of the two brain hemispheres—feminine (right) and masculine (left). The evidence appears to indicate that early writings were produced using both hemispheres. However, this did not entail true self-consciousness. The right brain was dominant. Thus, volition, planning, and initiative were organized in such a way that it was internally "*told* to the individual in his familiar language, sometimes with the visual aura of a familiar friend or authority figure or 'god', or sometimes as a voice alone. The individual obeyed these...voices because he could not *see* what to do by himself."[51]

The experience just described is similar to what we refer to today as *intuition* or *ESP* experienced by normal healthy people, as well as the *hallucinations* of mentally ill patients, though these differ in quality. The 'voice' or 'vision' is a right brain experience. The instances of God speaking through Moses and the Hebrew prophets, as well as the 'gods' referred to in the epics of the Greeks and others, were actually this type of right brain activity. Jaynes asserts that this experience usually occurs in times of stress even today.[52]

In chapter one, we considered the role that chaos, in the form of natural disasters, played in the extinction of species, notably the dinosaurs. And, in chapter two, we note Leaky's reference to similar causes for the evolutionary shifts in the development of humanity. Likewise, Jaynes believes that catastrophes of various kinds were the chief contributors to the awakening of consciousness. Furthermore, he holds that natural selection has played only a minor role, and without the catastrophic interventions, would probably have had little or no effect.

"The second millennium B.C.E. was heavy laden with profound and irreversible changes. Vast geological catastrophes occurred. Civilizations perished. Half the world's population became refugees."[53] Invasions of warring groups, particularly Assyria, volcanic eruptions and earthquakes, and the vast migrations of peoples created massive stresses on humanity that forced an awakening of consciousness. With the invention of writing, especially the alphabet, civilizations desired to record their experience for the benefit of succeeding generations. All of this accelerated the collapse of the bicameral mind and reinforced the dominance of the masculine left brain.

Jaynes notes that "the coming of consciousness can in a certain vague sense be construed as a shift from an auditory mind to a visual mind." This shift appears to be seen for the first time in the Greek epic, the Iliad, though there are still *voices* referred to as gods. The Iliad seems to indicate the beginning of the recognition of personal accountability and responsibility. But it is only later, with the writings of the Greek philosophers, especially Plato, that the concept of *knowing oneself* began to create the *dualism* which has become the central problem of consciousness that is still with us today. Dualism separates the subjective self from the objective world.

We referred to the Habiru or Hebrews earlier in this chapter. Jaynes contends that their story, which has come down to us as the Old Testament, "is in its grand overall contour the description of the loss of the bicameral mind, and its replacement by subjectivity over the first millennium B.C.E."[54] While much of the Hebrew Bible, particularly the first books, is believed to have been gathered and woven together from the writings of other places, peoples, and periods, other books are considered to be *pure,* in the sense that they are mostly what they say they are and can be accurately dated. Two of these books clearly illustrate Jaynes' thesis regarding the bicameral mind. The oldest is *Amos,* dating from the 8th century B.C.E., and the most recent is *Ecclesiastes,* from the 2nd century B.C.E. Jaynes asserts that there is an authentic difference between a bicameral man in *Amos,* and a subjective conscious man in *Ecclesiastes.*

In *Amos,* the prophet uses no words for mind, think, feel, understand, or anything similar. Amos never ponders anything in his heart. He can't; he would not know what it meant. *Ecclesiastes* is the opposite in every way. The author ponders things as deeply in his heart as possible. He thinks, considers, compares one thing with another, and uses brilliant metaphors in the process. Amos uses external divination, is "fiercely righteous, absolutely assured, nobly rude, and speaks a blistering god-speech." The author of *Ecclesiastes* never uses external divination. He "would be an excellent fireside friend, mellow, kindly, concerned, hesitant, surveying all of life in a way that would have been impossible for Amos."[55]

Fields of Influence

In chapters 1 and 2 we discussed how all the many kinds of living organisms, as well as humanity itself, have come into being through a vast creative process. These are all products of evolution, which continues at an ever-accelerating pace, especially with humanity. Societies, cultures, civilizations, economies, science and technology also evolve. Rupert Sheldrake, a British biochemist, offers insight into the mechanism by which this occurs.

According to Sheldrake, a scientific hypothesis known as *formative causation,* extending back to biologists in the 1920s, postulates that the nature of things depends on what is called *morphic fields* (fields of form). These fields are similar to the gravitational, electro-magnetic, and strong and weak nuclear fields known to physics.

> "Morphic fields, like the fields of physics, are non-material regions of influence extending in space and continuing in time. They are localized within and around the systems they organize. When any particular organized system ceases to exist...as when an animal dies, its organizing

field disappears from that place. But in another sense, morphic fields do not disappear: they are *potential* organizing patterns of influence, and can appear again physically in other times and places, wherever and whenever the physical conditions are appropriate. When they do so, they contain within themselves a memory of their previous physical existences."[56]

Morphic resonance is the process by which the past becomes present in morphic fields. The transmission of formative causal influences resonates through both space and time because the memory within morphic fields is cumulative. Thus, all sorts of behavioral patterns, whether in living or non-living beings, become habitual through repetition. Until the 1960s, the known fields of physics were assumed to be governed by eternal, unchangeable laws of nature. In contrast, morphic fields are known to arise and *evolve* in time and space, influenced by conditions in the world around them. Today, the science of theoretical physics is in ferment, so that physicists are recognizing that their concepts are reaching back to the first moments of creation. New and evolutionary theories regarding matter and fields have come into being.

None of the fields of physics is reducible to any of the others. The same is true of the morphic fields, especially the *morphogenetic* fields, which can induce (generate) new forms (morpho-) that govern the process of behavioral change in organisms and help to rearrange their normal organizing development into new patterns. Morphogenetic fields also guide the processes of regulation and regeneration after an organism has sustained some kind of damage. They are essential for healing. Each living species contains and subsists in its own morphogenetic field. In fact, each organism's morphogenetic field appears to contain an entire hierarchy of fields which organize various aspects of the development and regeneration of that organism. And these fields have likewise evolved.

It appears that morphogenetic fields contain an inherent memory that is immanent in organisms. They evolve *within* the realm of nature and are influenced by what has happened before. Habits build up within them. This theory of morphogenetic fields is in agreement with what we have already described about the *innate* quality of evolutionary programming, compounded by the outside influences which impinge upon the organism.

The assumption that morphogenetic fields are physically real, in the sense that the fields of physics are physically real, is the basis for the hypothesis of formative causation. It postulates a two-way flow of influence from fields to organisms and from organisms to fields. However, these fields are not seen as the transmission of energy so much, but rather as merely influence. The view is that all nature is evolutionary because of these fields

So how does this hypothesis illuminate what we have already said regarding human evolution? Sheldrake quotes another theorist:

> "Investigations point towards a compelling idea, that all nature is ultimately controlled by the activities of a single *superforce*. The superforce would have the power to bring the universe into being and furnish it with light, energy, matter, and structure. But the superforce would amount to more than just a creative agency. It would represent an amalgamation of matter, space-time, and force into an integrated and harmonious framework that bestows upon the universe a hitherto unsuspected unity.»[57]

To me, this passage expresses the idea of Divine Wisdom at work, as described by a modern physicist. In fact, Sheldrake even refers to this superforce as the Great Mother Goddess.[58] To him "it makes sense to think of the entire universe as an all-inclusive organism." From this viewpoint, the entire universe would have a morphic field which would include, influence, and interconnect the morphic fields of all the organisms within it. Finally, he postulates that the assumption of the hypothesis of *formative causation,* that morphic resonance takes place *only* from the past, may be wrong. It may emanate from the future as well, or even instead.

Summary

In this chapter we have discussed several approaches to understanding the evolution of humanity, from theorists of various disciplines. I recognize an important continuity throughout these viewpoints that goes beyond the former mechanistic theories of physics as well as the Darwinian idea of natural selection.

My rationale for tracing the evolutionary pattern in this chapter and the preceding chapters is in preparation for furthering the discussion of human evolution as it is presenting itself now in the 21st century. Today we are witnessing the formation of a more balanced consciousness, which includes the frequent use of the feminine right brain. We will discuss this in a later chapter.

CHAPTER FOUR
Evolution or Devolution?

The state of our consciousness these days is very troubled. Our relationships are in difficulty, our government has become more and more corrupt, our churches are failing us, and the financial market has brought many people to economic ruin. I believe there is a common thread in all of these debilitating developments. It is the current lack of critical thinking and the apathetic *devolution* of mankind's state of consciousness.

Still, things are changing for a considerable number of people, albeit subtly. There is a "new consciousness" afoot, and it is attracting more and more individuals and groups. My sense is that the tipping point into the transformation of human consciousness to the next level will be initiated when a critical mass of similar thinkers has been reached. Human beings, in general, will experience a new and more mature sense of reality and peace.

So I will be addressing human evolution in a new way, as the formation of cultural changes effected by critical, *contemplative* thinkers who are choosing to reformulate their relationships with themselves, other persons, their community, nature, and God. By contemplation I am not referring to what monks do in their cloisters. Rather, I am recommending a serious evaluation of oneself and one's ideas so as to remedy what is not viable any longer in one's lifestyle. I expect that this process, when shared with others, will bring new ideas into the cultural milieu. But before we can discuss this matter I want to present in greater detail what needs to be reevaluated. Consequently, I need to reiterate some of the material already briefly discussed in chapters 2 and 3.

Patriarchy Revisited

Previously I noted that the patriarchal system was introduced into the human experience by foreign invaders who conquered and occupied peaceful European and Middle Eastern cultures in which women had been respected and honored. In chapter 3 we discussed how the invaders' worship of masculine gods gradually brought about the demise of goddess worship and ultimately resulted in the suppression of women over the centuries.

Nevertheless, patriarchy has been responsible for many positive gifts to human society. Literacy, science, and technology would not have become part of western culture without the development and predominance of the masculine left brain that opened those areas to us. But there are two negative aspects of patriarchy, which were introduced from the onset—*misogeny* and *terrorism*. We shall consider these two aspects in detail.

Misogyny has been called the world's oldest prejudice. But now, in our "relatively enlightened age," we have finally come to recognize that the phenomenon of misogyny has been identified not only as a source of oppression and injustice toward women, but also as an obstacle to human development, and to social and economic progress. This recognition presents an opportunity to discover the ways in which our consciousness can evolve further in order to better the human condition.

Growing up in Belfast, Northern Ireland, Jack Holland[59] soon learned that though "men would step in to defend a dog from being kicked around by another man," there was no obligation "to do the same when faced with brutality being inflicted on a wife by her husband." This attitude prevailed because it was assumed that a "sacred status" existed in the relationship between man and wife, which barred intervention. Hatred coexists with desire in such a peculiar way that it makes misogyny very complex. It involves a man's conflict with himself, and for the most part it is not even recognized. A man needs a woman, yet looks upon her with derision or contempt.

The issue of misogyny developed a more interesting and devastating outlook for Christian women, especially Catholics, in the Middle Ages, when the Church gradually proclaimed Mary, the Mother of Jesus, as Queen of heaven, the *Theotokos* or God-bearer, and later as the Immaculate Conception. Here was a woman who was defined as:

> born sinless, maintaining that state throughout her life, was a virgin before, during, and after the birth of Jesus, and remained meek, humble, and obedient to God for her entire life.

This elevated her above both men and women, and literally took her out of the realm of ordinary human experience, yet would not allow her to be considered divine in any way. She is known as the Mother of God and Queen of Heaven, but not as the Great Mother Goddess.

Worse still, women were expected to view Mary as a role model. Her sexlessness was a rebuke to female sexuality. Her obedience encouraged the belief that the norms of patriarchal society in regard to social relationships represented divine sanction. Mary was deemed to be human yet raised to *near* divinity. In fact, she could not be seen as *either* truly human or divine. Mary was described in such a way that ordinary women could not identify with her. The only way that a woman could possibly hope to emulate the Virgin Mother was to forget about her sexuality.

Because for much of human history misogyny was considered "the common sense of society," present in all the world's major religions, and touted by the world's most renowned philosophers, women became complicit in believing their second-rate status. The conventional history of women consists largely of the history of their relationship to men and, until very recently, in relation to very little else.

Wartime is especially traumatic for women. Traditionally, rape in wartime is the least punished offense. In the early 1990s, during the wars in the former Yugoslavia, the Serbian authorities established rape camps, where Moslem and Croatian women were systematically raped and deliberately impregnated. But women began campaigning to redress this injustice. "In 1993, at the UN conference on human rights held in Vienna, rape and other forms of sexual violence were recognized as war crimes...Realistically, the only way to abolish rape during war is to abolish war."[60]

This type of violence has continued, however, in parts of Africa where there is civil war. It is estimated that a woman is raped every 17 seconds in South Africa. And in Saudi Arabia and other countries that practice Moslem sharia law, if a woman is raped there is a likelihood that a male family member will perform an "honor killing" on her because her virginity had been violated, or if married, because she was deemed to be an adulteress.

The interesting and hopeful fact is that not all men are misogynists. Misogyny is merely a part of woman's relationship to man. The progress that women have made towards equality in Western or Western-style democracies over the last two centuries has *only* been achieved with the advocacy and support of men.

Of my five grown children, four are male. Their wives all have full-time jobs. The two oldest sons were married in their late forties and their wives are unable to bear children for medical reasons. The two younger sons, who have children, have both confessed to me that they "love being Mr. Mom." All of our sons are in the process of acquiring full partnership equality with their wives. It is very obvious.

Yet, many women, even on issues involving women's rights, have been on the side of men who have opposed these rights, including the right to vote. History proves that women can be as pro-war as men, even though the lives of their husbands and sons are at stake. And women sometimes incite violence against other women.

Evolution denies that humankind stands apart from nature and the natural processes that shaped the rest of the living world. The overwhelming evidence is that human behavior is shaped by inherited characteristics as well as by social factors. We are a product of evolution and that includes our sexual behavior. We are different, both as men and women, and as individuals, and Darwin's theory does not impose any moral or legal discrimination based on differences. By recognizing the function of differences between the sexes, evolutionary theory can defend us against those who want to ignore or eradicate the differences, and thereby do violence to human nature.[61]

After all is said and done, "what we call *history* is merely the tale that patriarchy wants to tell, and misogyny is its ideology."[62] The hatred of women strikes at our innermost selves, whether male or female. It is only by achieving equality between the sexes that we will eventually be able to banish misogyny and put an end to that prejudice. This is the time for us to write her-story.

Terrorism

Holland stated that men are conflicted, in their relationships with women, between their sexual desire and their "need" to dominate. He also implied that there is a connection between sexuality and war and terrorism. Morgan[63] goes even further and maintains that male sexuality is at the *root* of terrorism. This is a hard saying at the very least. Yet, when we look at the cross-cultural pattern we see that what forms the central core of terrorism is the intersection of violence, eroticism, and what is considered "masculinity." We need to change the definition of "manhood" that is *toxic* to men and *lethal* to women. Together, as men and women, we can change it, but it is not a simple task.

"The ultimate sexual idol of a male-centered cultural tradition that stretches from pre-Biblical times to the present" is the logical extension of the patriarchal hero/martyr. Depending on your point of view, this can be the terrorist or the freedom fighter, and many varieties in between. Morgan sees the hero/martyr as the Demon Lover, and she notes that society is secretly or openly fascinated by him. He is an ideal type of self-sacrifice, volatility, purity, and severe discipline. We are told that women lust to have him, and men long to *be* him. Now he stalks among us so that we are a people really in the grips of post-traumatic stress syndrome. [64]

Politics, which represents a struggle for power, frequently resorts to violence to obtain power. But because power and violence are actually opposites, violence tends to appear only when power is jeopardized, and over time will result in the disappearance of power. Morgan says:

"The terrorist mystique is twin brother to the manhood mystique—and the mythic father of both is the hero. The

> terrorist has charisma *because* he is the technological-age
> manifestation of the hero...He is the Hero Triumphant
> when he wins his revolution and moves into the presi-
> dential palace...and he is the Hero Martyred when he
> loses and is destroyed...Because he carries within him
> the double potential of triumphal power and sacrificial
> power, he personifies in patriarchal terms all that remains
> to us—after centuries of manipulation, diminution, and
> corruption—of what once was *passion.*"[65]

This explains why terrorists like Osama bin Laden and others are seen by
so many as a hero. They are passionate about their "mission" and carrying it forward is essential to their identity and self esteem. Fundamentalist
Muslims, in particular, view such a passion as divinely inspired.

The Judeo-Christian tradition split the concept of passion into the
acceptable (passion for God) and the unacceptable (earthly or carnal passion). Though Morgan believes that the male hero and his passionate quest
are not representative of most men, nevertheless, she questions "whether
most men notice and realize *that.*" Or does each man, secretly or openly,
identify with the hero? Even for the average man, a daily dose of power
over someone else's life appears to be desired, if not deemed necessary.

Essentially, Morgan's work is a feminist analysis of the violence which
manifests as the phenomenon of terrorism, often called "the politics of last
resort." She clearly states the necessity for women, the majority of humanity, to "address and engage the issue" or it will "never be understood, much
less solved."[66] At last, a transformative wave is emerging which promises to
address it—*women have become a global political force.*

Morgan refers to compartmentalization, or the institutionalization of
disconnection, as the one quality which manifests the "genius of patriarchy."
On the other hand, the "genius of feminism," its thought, culture, and
action, is *connectivity.* This involves both attentiveness and recognition, and
is an activist technique for being in the world and for changing it.[67]

Discussions with women from various walks of life, including a four-
hour interview with Patricia Hearst, while she was in prison, have convinced Morgan that women are bred to please, most especially in the case

of the privileged rich. Many women find it difficult to be curious or feel deeply about anything, or sense that they may have a unique purpose in life. I also found this to be true of the women I interviewed.

A woman is the only qualified expert on her own existence. There are things she knows she does not know about herself. These are things which are known to her subconsciously, which *must* become familiar to her if she is to live her life to the full. She needs her lifetime in order to teach herself what she knows in her subconscious. There is a silence that *will* not speak and a silence that *may* not speak. The latter refers to the silence that is kept "for the sake of peace," by which a woman does violence against herself. If she remains in this silence it is an active violence. This silence, born out of fear, begets terror if it is not dissolved. To Morgan, "the sole source of fear...is the loss or theft of *consciousness* while still alive, a death-in-life that *is* 'the fate worse than death'."[68] Yet we manufacture fear faster and more often than any other emotion.

Another area of human behavior that promotes fear is the violence increasingly acted out by children. Allan Guggenbuhl,[69] a Jungian analyst who has studied this phenomenon in Switzerland, claims that it is prevalent from kindergarten throughout the school years. Among younger children violence is an individual problem, whereas in elementary and high school it becomes a group problem, frequently with gangs.

Because the root of violence is fear, which can take many forms, there is a search for some kind of *security* in an attempt to allay the fear. And violence often appears to be the solution. Among younger children, it is the teacher and the parents who must take charge to seek out the cause of the problem. But by the elementary and high school years, once the violence has escalated to the group, the situation becomes much more complex. The influence of the peer group has taken over, and in many cases parents become very fearful of their children. This scenario tells us that there is something very wrong with our world.

One factor in this situation, according to Guggenbuhl,[70] is the change in the parent-child relationship within the last generation. No longer are the parents the moral teachers and roll models that existed in former generations. Instead the boundaries between parent and child have loosened. Parents now want to be more involved with their children's activities, and, on the other hand, more willing to allow the children to make their own choices. This tends to give mixed messages to the child and frequently generates anger and secrecy, as well as fear of discovery.

Peer groups among children with similar issues can easily lead to bullying or to the formation of gangs which lead to overt violence. Two of the central factors in this situation are the possession and use of weapons and rampant drug abuse. Weapons perpetrate violence on others, while the use of illegal drugs causes violence to the self, frequently resulting in suicide, the ultimate act of self violence. While we have become very aware of the dangers involved with violence in children, we do not yet have a genuine solution for it. The gradual breakdown of the patriarchal power system, has yet to teach us about a remedy. Currently, the only way to address it appears to be crisis intervention.

Morgan notes that collectively, regarding violence among both children and adults, our actions have been more reactive than active. She believes that women, as the human *majority,* because they are increasingly insisting on their own *empowerment,* can "utterly change the terms on which power is held or seized, on which the world is sustained or destroyed."[71] We will develop this idea further in a later chapter.

Evolutionary Chaos Once More

Because the patriarchal system has reached its maximum absurdity, and is breaking down, we have created world-wide chaos. This includes military engagement between nations, job insecurity in our corporations, scandals within our religious traditions, corruption in our financial system, and strained relationships within the family.

I have noted the necessity of chaos for the evolutionary process in the previous chapters. Natural selection is not sufficient for bringing about evolutionary change. Chaotic conditions give the process an extra boost, yet do not deny the presence of gradual change as well. Moreover, Sheldrake's[72] concept of morphogenetic fields, impinging on current conditions, whether from the known past or the yet unknown future, offers a hypothesis for the manner in which evolutionary transformations take place. I also noted that, ultimately, chaos proves to be just as "orderly" as longer, seemingly more stable periods.

An old saying is "history repeats itself." This is certainly true of *homo sapiens* in recent centuries. But then, the history of mankind, compared to the four and one-half billion year history of our planet, is very brief. We have little information concerning how stable the lengthy periods actually were between the cataclysms that permanently changed everything. Were there repetitive cycles in these periods? It's difficult to know; yet we do have information about repetitive cycles in *human* history, especially regarding the Western world.

William Strauss, a political analyst, and Neil Howe, an economist and historian, have presented a viewpoint[73] which, I believe, sheds considerable light on repetitive cycles and the chaotic conditions of our age. They have discovered historical patterns that recur over time, which describe the natural rhythms of social experience. I believe these rhythms can be classified as morphogenetic fields.

The evidence they present covers the last five centuries in Anglo-American society, in which a new *turning* occurs every two decades or so. "At the start of each *turning,* people change how they feel about themselves, the culture, the nation, and the future." Turnings occur in cycles of four, which span the length of a long human life of at least eighty years or longer, and comprise history's seasonal rhythm of growth, maturation, decay, and destruction.

The authors describe it this way:

> The *First Turning* is a *High,* an upbeat era of strengthening institutions and weakening individualism, when a new civic order implants and the old-values regime decays.

> The *Second Turning* is an *Awakening,* a passionate era of spiritual upheaval, when the civic order comes under attack from a new-values regime.

> The *Third Turning* is an *Unraveling,* a downcast era of strengthening individualism and weakening institutions, when the old civic order decays and the new-values regime implants.

> The *Fourth Turning* is a *Crisis,* a decisive era of secular upheaval, when the values regime propels the replacement of the old civic order with a new one.[74]

The authors predicted in 1997 that the next fourth turning would begin around 2005. It certainly was in the developing process even though we were not aware of it until 200809. Looking back over our history we can see that 80 years have passed since the Great Depression began with the "crash" of the Stock Market. Roughly 80 years before that, we were leading up to the Civil War. And 80 years prior, we were in the midst of revolting against Britain and leading up to the Revolutionary War. That particular fourth turning eventually brought about our independence and the writing of our constitution. What is even more significant today is that, because of globalization, the eighty year cycle of turnings *now* affects the entire planet. Our history is intimately involved with and connected to that of every other nation on earth.

Strauss and Howe's 1997 predictions, which they listed at the end of the unraveling of a third turning, concern our present Crisis and include:[75]

- Political and economic implosion;
- Genuine hardship with severe distress that could involve questions of class, race, and nation;
- Seeds of social rebirth;
- Regret about recent mistakes and a resolute new consensus about what to do;
- Possibility of an eruption of insurrection or civil violence;
- High risk of war, especially nuclear war;
- A unique opportunity to achieve a new greatness as a people.
- So far they are right on the mark. During this current fourth turning we will continue to need both personal sacrifice and public authority. The authors comment:

- "History warns that when a Crisis catalyzes, a previously dominant political party can find itself directly blamed for perceived 'mistakes' that led to the national emergency. Whoever holds power when the Fourth Turning arrives could...find itself out of power for a generation. Key persons associated with it could find themselves defamed, stigmatized, harassed, economically ruined, personally punished—or worse."[76]
- Civic virtue is frequently lost in a fourth turning, but just as frequently regained.

Though a crisis mood renders desperation in society, it also provides a means for new capability, which is why this "winter" cycle should be welcomed as much as feared. It brings the chaos that can promote an evolutionary transformation for society. This Crisis necessitates the death and rebirth of the social order. No one can predict the outcome in advance. Classic virtues that have been held sacred in the past may not necessarily pay off in the Unraveling—traits like trust, reliability, patience, perseverance, thrift, and selflessness—but will be sorely needed in the Crisis.

The authors list a number of necessary steps concerning what needs to be implemented during this fourth turning:[77]

Rectify: Return to the classic virtues.
Converge: Heed emerging community norms.
Bond: Build personal relationships of all kinds.
Gather: Prepare yourself and your children for teamwork.
Root: Look to your family for support.
Brace: Gird for the weakening or collapse of public support mechanisms.
Hedge: Diversify everything you do.

In this way a fourth turning allows a society's survival instincts to emerge, allowing it to work through problems that otherwise might destroy it. Everyone needs to become aware and to sacrifice for whatever is necessary to bring this about. No one can afford to be *clueless* any longer.

Summary

We have examined the chief factors, patriarchal misogyny and terrorism, which have contributed to the crisis of our time. Though these factors have been present for many centuries, they have reached a threshold that has broken into chaos. We are finally in a position of sufficient awareness that can set us on track for an evolutionary breakthrough. But we *must* choose to cooperate with the morphogenetic fields that are being presented. Both the past and future offer us an opportunity to change our present conditions.

Chapter Five
Human Evolution Over the Individual Lifespan

We have discussed the evolutionary evidence concerning the natural world and the development of consciousness in the previous chapters. I wish to continue this process in regard to the evolution of each human being throughout his or her lifespan. It begins with the genetic programming stemming from the sexual union of parental genes. But the genetic makeup from the combined DNA is not sufficient to create the person one is meant to become. I believe there is a spiritual component which evolves as well, that is probably *not* encoded in the DNA.

During the nine months of gestation the developing fetus is subjected to many experiences which set the stage for later development. It then continues after birth with the embeddedness in the family of origin, the original and basic *culture* for each person. The effects of education, religious training (or none at all), the experience with one's peer group, and other influences, continue to accumulate throughout the lifespan. All of these environmental influences involve physical and spiritual relationships with others. In this way a life trajectory develops in which the person learns to discern his/her unique possibilities, which are the best suited to that person, and those that offer opportunities for optimal success. And *chaos* will appear as pain and suffering when it is needed to boost the appropriate choices.

PATRICIA KRAUS, PH.D.

Finding My Own Path

In my early developmental years I learned that boys and girls seemed to have different *roles* in life, even though we attended the same schools and had the same female teachers. I had to learn to sew, cook, clean the house, do laundry, and baby-sit. And I was not allowed to question my father's authority. My brothers had to learn to mow grass in the summer and to shovel snow in the winter. My father told me he would not send me to college, even though I was the best student among the three of us. He would see to it that my brothers attended college, however. His logic was that I would marry one day and a college education would be wasted. I now understand his unspoken explanation to mean, that if I were to marry and have children, it was my *duty to stay home* and care for my husband and children—a typical patriarchal definition of woman's major, perhaps even only, role in life.

It was my father's decision to send me to business school instead. My mother had attended business school instead of high school, and my father figured that if she could get an important job so could I. After six weeks in business school I realized I was a total misfit. Because my relationship with my mother was very close, she respected me as a person and supported my decision to leave the school and to continue my higher education.

I took an office job as a filing clerk for a year in order to save money to pay my college tuition. A year later I entered college as a freshman and by the end of that year I was offered a part-time position in the chemistry department as an office clerk for the duration of my education in chemistry, physics and mathematics. Eventually my job led to library and laboratory research. I was the only female in my science program with 15 males. During those years I *never felt oppressed* as a woman, because I was able to find ways to follow my dreams due to my mother's love and support. She was always there to encourage me.

When I met my husband-to-be, a doctoral student in the chemistry department, I realized that he respected me and my pursuits. He frequently stated that I should probably continue on to graduate school at some point in the future. When many women in my generation began to voice their opinions about being oppressed and in need of liberation, (especially after Betty Friedan's [78] first book was published) I always responded that I was liberated already. It would be almost thirty years before I read her book. By then I felt as though she had written the story of my life.

A new understanding of our "culture" slowly began to occur to me—that it is really composed of two cultures—one male, one female. Harkening back to how my brothers and I were differentially socialized as children, I recognized that, like my mother, I was taught to function in relation to others—their comfort, their wishes, their pleasure. My brothers were taught to function for the sake of things—mowing the lawn, shoveling the snow—and their own wishes and pleasures. And they were expected to go out into the world, and to find satisfactory employment that would compete with others, so that when they married, they would be able to pay the bills for their wives, children and households.

At times, as a child, I had wished I were a boy, and that I would not have to stay home every Saturday helping my mother clean our house. But I was expected to marry and to stay in the home, and so I needed to experience how to manage these duties. This was the role which was expected of young women of my generation, very few of whom had gone to college.

My conflict was that I wanted to go out to work and achieve, as well as marry and start a family. This would require two different modes of self-expression. I would need to compete and achieve in the work world, but to cooperate and collaborate on the home front. I compromised and chose to work for a few years before starting the family I dearly desired. It seemed a practical solution until I found myself feeling "trapped" during our children's teenage years.

My husband was a good provider, intelligent, refined, a kind man. There was only one fly in the ointment—he and I could not adequately communicate about household tasks or the problems with our children. I could not understand why he did not see that I was truly in need of help. His mother had been the central figure in his family, for him and his brother, and I believe he thought that was my duty, also. However, with five children I felt overwhelmed, because I was the only parent to discipline them and meet their daily needs. And it gradually became a "macho" world with the onset of our four boys' teenage years. They needed their father's example and mentoring, something he did not seem to understand. I was also determined that I would not subject our daughter to the kind of rigid *homemaker* routine to which I had been subjected.

Our marriage was suffering and one of our sons was very troubled with emotional issues due to attention deficit-hyperactive syndrome. We eventually went to family therapy, and at this point I decided to return to graduate school, switching from the "hard science" education of my youth in order to train as a family therapist. I learned a great deal from our therapy, as well as my theoretical and counselor training. This eventually became a continual search for answers regarding gender issues. My years of training as a family therapist and working with clients, followed by research in the field of spirituality, and training as a spiritual director, led to my doctoral research on continuing human development in adulthood. I began to study the connection between culture, human relationships, and ongoing spiritual and personal development. The research in the field of developmental psychology seemed to be the direction for me. I did not realize at the time that this research represented the twentieth century approach to the *evolution* of the individual self during the lifespan. Nor did I understand that I was undergoing my own evolution.

Developmental Theorists

I came upon the research of Carol Gilligan[79] and Robert Kegan[80], who had both studied under Lawrence Kohlberg[81] in the field of moral development. All three of these theorists presented clear evidence of ongoing human development beyond that of early adulthood. The basic shortcoming of Kohlberg's research on moral development is that he studied only males.

Carol Gilligan intuitively saw that females develop differently from males because of the ways in which they are socialized in the family and peer group. Determined to discover the ways in which this occurs, she examined the work of Nancy Chodorow[82], who attributed male and female developmental differences to "the fact that women, universally, are largely responsible for early child care." Because this early social environment is experienced differently by male and female children, basic sex differences occur, and recur in succeeding generations, regarding personality development. As a result "in any given society, feminine personality comes to define itself in relation and connection to other people more than masculine personality."[83] Chodorow believed that this *difference* is firmly and irreversibly established for both sexes by the time a child is around age three.

Because the primary caretaker for both sexes is typically female, a girl's identity formation takes place in a context of ongoing relationship and identification with her mother. "Mothers tend to experience their daughters as more alike, and continuous with themselves." And girls experience themselves like their mothers. Likewise, mothers experience their sons as different from themselves, and boys, in defining themselves as masculine, as separate from their mothers. Consequently, girls emerge from this period with a tendency toward empathy built into their primary definition of self, whereas boys do not. On the other hand, male development entails more defensive and firmer ego boundaries.

Gilligan was determined to follow up on Chodorow's thesis. She designed a research protocol, called the *Rights and Responsibilities Study,* in which she explored differing views of morality and understanding of the self for both men and women. Her aim was to uncover, especially, the apparent puzzles that pertain to women's identity formation and moral development in adolescence and adulthood, and how they differed from males. (See Appendix A)

A case in point is the way aggression as a response to danger is experienced by men and women. Gilligan's findings suggest that men and women perceive danger in different social situations, and construe danger in different ways. Men tend to see danger more often in close personal relationship than in achievement, construing danger to arise from intimacy. The danger of intimacy is felt to be one of entrapment or betrayal, being caught in a smothering relationship, or humiliated by rejection and deceit. On the contrary, women perceived danger in impersonal achievement situations, construing danger to result from competitive success. This danger is experienced as a fear of isolation, that in standing out or being set apart by success, they will be left alone.[84]

Sometime later Gilligan studied girls, ages 9 to 16, who were attending a private school. She found that 9 or 10 year old girls were very honest about themselves. By the time they reached 12 or 13, when asked what they thought about almost anything, they answered, "I don't know," again and again. Gilligan's solution to this puzzle was that something had happened to change their sense of self. She concluded that it was the girls' *inner voice* that "stands up for what they believe" about themselves that had been buried.[85]

Gilligan realized that it was the onset of received cultural messages that had caused this change. She also studied boys in the same age range and found that they seemed to bury their inner voices as early as age four. Her conclusion was that this was the work of a patriarchal society already imposing the stereotypical ideas about femininity and masculinity.

Gilligan's research findings of essential differences in the way men and women experience and describe themselves have been verified and illuminated through research in another area. Deborah Tannen, a professor of linguistics at Georgetown University, has analyzed the way men and women use language in interpersonal communication. In theme after theme, and chapter after chapter of her book[86], she has shown how men and women differ in their approach. Her conclusion is that they "just don't understand" each other's experience.

The research of women like Chodorow, Gilligan, and Tannen, sheds new light on male and female differences. Previously, the "truths" of psychological theory, largely held by men, had blinded psychologists to the *truth* of women's experience. Images of hierarchy for men, and those of "web" and connection for women, convey different ways of structuring relationships, and are associated with different views of morality and self. They inform different modes of assertion and response. For men it is the wish to be alone at the top and the consequent fear that others will get too close. And for women, the wish to be at the center of connection, generates the consequent fear of being too far out on the edge.[87]

Innate Biological Differences

The research presented above refers to female and male differences which result from stereotypical notions resulting from interaction with our culture. On the other hand, there are a number of *innate* differences between men and women, over and above the relational and cultural ones reported by Gilligan and others, which are inherent in the X and Y genes inhabiting our DNA. The ramifications of this genetic difference extend all the way from external physical characteristics, to hormonal differences. More recently, the discovery of considerable variation between men and women in the size of areas of the brain illustrates that there is an *inborn* inclinational variance.[88] These brain variations differentially affect men and women in several ways: emotionally, in their behavioral preferences, and in their reactions to stress, and so forth. Nevertheless, there is ample evidence that these differences in the human brain have developed over the millennia in both men and women.

Evidence from archeological, anthropological, and historical research, previously described in chapter 3, reveals massive cultural change stemming from the development over time of language, methods of writing, and finally the invention of the alphabet.[89] These developments have altered human consciousness, which in turn has brought about additional changes in the brains of both men and women.

Though Gilligan and Kegan both did their research under the same mentor, they approached human development in very different ways. Kegan also studied both men and women, but used a developmental *stage* design similar to Kohlberg. Many developmental theorists, including Erikson[90], Maslow[91], and Piaget[92] have observed how human beings proceed through a number of stages, beginning in infancy and progressing through adolescence, young adulthood, mid-life, and all the way into old age.

Kegan followed the developmental pattern described by Piaget. He viewed this process as an emotional (affective) development as well as an intellectual (cognitive) one. He began to re-conceptualize Piaget's theory, and to refer to his own view as the theory of the *evolving self.* Kegan came to believe that "if you want to understand another person in some fundamental way you must know where the person is in his or her *evolution.*"

This entails a lifelong process of evolution or adaptation "in the sense of an active process of increasingly organizing the relationship of the self to the environment." He referred to this as "the master motion in personality." He saw that "the state of a person's evolution is so crucial to understanding him or her...because the way in which the person is settling the issue of what is *self* and what is *other* essentially defines the underlying logic of the person's meanings."[93]

Kegan referred to infancy as stage 0 in his approach (K-0).[94] The child has begun its *evolution* outside the womb merged with its caretakers—holding, feeding, physical care, and so forth. But by age two the child's sense of self has begun to shift and become embedded in his or her own impulses and perceptions. (See Appendix B for further discussion.)

In the years between two and six, the child enters some type of formal education, and begins to formulate roles with parents, teachers, peers, and siblings. At this stage (K-1) the child will discuss her relationships with others primarily in terms of actions. These relationships with others, as the child begins the shift to K-2 are evaluated by the child in terms of feelings linked to reward or punishment.

As adolescence approaches, a shift from stage 2 toward stage 3 becomes noticeable, usually between the ages of 12 and 16. Like Piaget, Kegan called this developmental phase "concrete operations" because it referred to the preoccupation with concrete sensory experience. The school and family are the chief areas of authority, and the child displays self-sufficiency, competence and role differentiation. The adolescent child experiences a growing desire to find ways to please friends and others, particularly among the peer group. Mutuality with one or two close friends becomes desirable.

According to Kegan, the K-3 stage needs to develop even beyond mutuality, interpersonal agreement, and cooperation into an understanding of oneself as a unique individual. In order to accomplish the transition from K-3 to K-4, a person must begin to emerge from a kind of *embeddedness* in interpersonal relationships, particularly those that have become co-dependent. Usually one or more crises will occur in one's longstanding relationships, which will begin to be seen as a need to know oneself more deeply as an individual. By reflecting specifically on one's own personal behavior, he or she begins to reject the "fusion" with others, which is a keynote of co-dependence, in order to take responsibility for his or her own initiatives and preferences.

Further development beyond K-4 involves emerging from embeddedness in one's behavioral system, and realizing that others have their own unique systems, too. Initially, movement from K-4 toward K-5 is experienced as a threat to the *self* that has been recently independently established. But gradually there is a growing ability to reflect as a *self-conscious self* rather than merely reflecting on a behavioral process.

My Research

Prior to developing my own research methodology I had served as research assistant to the chairman of my doctoral committee. While on sabbatical, he had conducted interviews with 100 men over age 70, from three groups in India (50 subjects representing Hindu, Muslim, and Sikh religions) and three groups in England (50 subjects from Protestant, Catholic, and Jewish religions). Together we were able to identify evolutionary differences in these men, and the effects these differences had on their religious beliefs. What was most noteworthy was that the more evolved a man appeared to be, the *less likely* his beliefs coincided with his early belief system. This was true for men from all six faith groups. Moreover, the more evolved men were more alike, in their values and the way they saw themselves, *across* all six groups, *regardless* of their religion.

The data from this study thoroughly intrigued me. I wanted to see if religious beliefs evolved with developmental changes in women. With this in mind I chose to study mid-life Catholic women over forty. All were practicing Catholics except one who had left her beliefs behind. Another was a fairly recent convert. Several of the remaining group had left the church for a time and then later returned. My reason for choosing this sample was the hope that I might discover something about the way women were attempting to emerge from societal norms into a healthy understanding of their own unique personhood. I also chose to study only

Catholic women because of the strongly patriarchal context their religion presented. (See Appendix C for a discussion of methodology.)

Research Findings

One of the findings from my research reflected the impression of *feminism* held by the women in my sample. Though the vast majority of them said they were very grateful to the women's movement, fully 80% of them absolutely refused to refer to themselves as feminists. They simply did not identify with what their *idea* of "feminists" had to say about themselves. Most of them viewed feminism as an aberration of women's ideals. Yet, when we discussed feminism from a Christian point of view—including equality between men and women, equal opportunity and equal pay, and freedom to choose one's own career—it became evident to them that feminism would profit all people, not just women.

Furthermore, nearly all the women in the study eventually admitted they were feminists from that perspective. The consensus was that true feminism was not about male-bashing or female domination, or doing things the way men do it, but rather, it is about freedom for all citizens, male and female, to find their own way and to develop to their own maximum potential. All of these women admitted that feminine values and their own natural womanly instincts were very important to them and necessary for the common good in society.

A second important theme that emerged from my research sample was the significance of women's relationships with other women. They relied on these relationships for advice, companionship, personal growth, healing, building and maintenance of kinship, creating solidarity, and many other areas of their lives. These findings confirmed those from other research studies,[95] and coincided with the previous finding on the women's movement and feminism. These two major themes have helped me to better understand the male/female culture that has developed over the centuries and is still with us today, most especially and *detrimentally* in African and Middle Eastern countries.

A third important theme was that the more evolved the women were shown to be in regard to the Kegan developmental perspective, the more my subjects had altered their impressions of Catholicism and Christianity in general. They had become capable of evaluating their religious beliefs and revising their self concept in accordance with that. This, of course, correlated with the findings from the men's study referred to above.

In order to gain further insight into this issue I interviewed a few men, all of whom I sensed were dealing with *at least* their K-2 to K-3 developmental shift. One of the men I contacted described his journey of self-discovery, particularly in his relationships with women. Referring to the power issues differentially found to be operating in the "gender war," he had come to realize that women in their own way were equally as powerful as men, and that this fact was "less visible because of its very different form." He called this the *gender co-dependent power-over matrix*. He notes that "we are co-dependently engaged with someone when we transact with them to get our needs met," but hide the truth about this from ourselves and each other.

Another man described how his wife continually complained that he was "not connected" to her or their four children. He and his wife eventually sought marital therapy in order to resolve this issue. Still, a third male interviewee spoke of the relationship between spouses as the most difficult to reconcile. He also recalled, how when his grown children called on the phone, he automatically assumed they wanted to speak with their mother. On one occasion when his son called, and he was about to bring his wife to the phone, the son said, "Dad, I want to talk to you."

All of these men, I felt sure, were well along on their shift to K-3, or even on the way to K-4. However, a number of my male clients were really struggling with understanding their relationships. They simply could not understand what cooperation or genuine collaboration meant. They were "fence sitters," typical stage K-2 development, unable to make any meaningful approach toward relational healing. One client in particular said that he felt he was "sitting on a raft in the middle of a lake" and could not move from there. Four of these clients have divorced. I heard similar stories from many of the women I interviewed concerning their husbands. There were also numerous accounts of the type of misunderstood communication between husbands and wives reported by Gilligan and Tannen.

Gender Co-dependence

As a result of these findings, I began to understand the gender issues more thoroughly and more accurately. It encompasses the cultural duality we experience today and have for centuries. When we take a historical perspective on the human race we see that women have always instinctively known the value and importance of nurturance, close relationships and the need to maintain family and extended kinship. These are characteristics which, no doubt, stem from the female X-genetic programming.

In the earliest days of the development of the human person and civilization, the feminine values dominated instinctively because they represented the human characteristics critical for survival. As we have discussed previously, both men and women, from the artifacts discovered of early peoples, seem to have lived in a manner that supported these values. But then something happened (a *fall from grace* perhaps?) when warring tribes brought conflict, weapons, and devastating conquest on the scene.

A so-called "division of labor" developed among the people, where women were expected to perform the nurturing and kinship duties, while men indulged in the more competitive areas, included hunting, exploration, and going to war. Thus, wars involving tribal power struggles, the search for acclaim and success in many fields of endeavor, and other types of competition, took prominence for men over nurturance, cooperation, kinship, and advocacy—a historical development that has endured for hundreds, of generations.

Over many thousands of years women did not *consciously* and sufficiently value the nurturing and relational characteristics of their feminine nature to assert themselves in society as a whole. As the human race evolved, the *instinctive* feminine nature remained, alongside the development of ego or self-consciousness. When women experienced their mothering characteristics, they realized the "rightness" of their role in society and the duty of women to socialize their daughters into these roles.

Men, on the other hand, due to the increasing separation of their societal roles from the family setting, became more and more assertive, even aggressive, in their pursuit of activities that seemed meaningful to them. These "competitive values" asserted by men dominated their lives. Though we might refer to this as the dominance of the "testosterone effect," the situation is considerably more complex.

We now recognize that changes in the socialization of males and females, producing variations in role behavior and divisions in labor, gradually altered the definitions of "appropriate" male and female behaviors over time, eventually leading to the *stereotypes* for male and female that we continue to see to the present day. But it has become increasingly evident in the last century that the chief effect has been to create a *gender co-dependency,* which distorts the full development of the *self* in both men and women.

These changes in socialization no doubt contributed to the development of brain differences between the genders. Accommodations that originally served human survival today are proving to be *a threat to our race.* I believe that in our generation the human brain is accommodating once again to a new consciousness, and that humanity is in a state of transition that could lead to either transformation or destruction. We have come to recognize the need to work with gender issues, and to better understand the nature of true masculinity and femininity.

The Kegan *evolutionary* approach to human development sheds some light on the gender co-dependency dilemma. It is now understood that competitive behavior represents a less mature stage of human development (K-2) than that characterized by relational and cooperative (K-3) values. Kegan's work recognizes that both male and female preadolescent and adolescent children exhibit competitive behavior. By their teen years, male children are primarily being socialized by their competitive peer group (K-2).

On the other hand, one of the most important functions that women perform in society is the building and maintaining of kinship. Without this function by women there would be no society or culture. Conceiving and birthing children is a biological function that takes place quite naturally and more or less instinctively. But building and maintaining kinship is a psycho-spiritual function that must be learned. The successful rearing of children requires the combination of the biological and kinship functions.

For most females kinship formation is learned in the family context from and with their mothers, aunts, grandmothers, and older sisters. This socialization process is necessary in order that they may reach the more mature relational stage in which shared and cooperative values and behaviors, which are necessary for child rearing and maintenance of kinship, are developed beyond the earlier competitive behaviors. The attainment of this K-3 developmental stage (Kegan's interpersonal level) is a necessary step for the development of kinship. Here sympathy is learned, setting the stage for the possibility of the later development of empathy toward those who may be very different. Women are capable of kinship not only in their families, but among friends and coworkers as well.

The stereotypical behavioral patterns of less mature, competitive (K-2) males and more mature, cooperative (K-3) females have been reinforced for thousands of years as normative. Though the "female culture" tended to socialize women at the more mature relational level, it also demanded that they *cooperate* with their less mature male companions, who would inevitably dominate them according to the competitive "male culture". There were benefits for both genders. Women could be present to their children, maintaining the home environment, preparing the meals, and planting the crops. Men could hunt for food, provide protection from warring neighbors, and perform other tasks, all of which necessarily took them away from the family.

My research, through the interviews I conducted with mid-life women and men, and their relationships with each other, indicates that the *majority* of women become locked into K-3, while the *majority* of men remain at K-2. I believe this is due to the prevalence of our cultural stereotypes, and I shall attempt to explain how and why this occurs. This situation represents what I see as the way our humanity has been caught in a trap of *so-called* "appropriate masculinity and femininity" for thousands of years.

In order to maintain a sense of cohesion between spouses, women have for hundreds of generations condoned and colluded with their husband's wishes and behaviors in order to meet their needs and those of their children. Women had their own needs met, especially for protection and other activities like trade and the acquisition of wealth. Thus they maintained the kinship even though their men lived on the periphery of the family system.

In the current stage of the development of technology, humanity realizes that it could destroy itself in many ways, not only with nuclear war, but also with other technical means, including the proliferation of diseases and chemical poisoning of all sorts. Consequently, the feminine values are needed more than ever in our day. In early 2004, I recall hearing an Iraqi man on television begging for more women to become involved in the government they were hoping to elect very soon. He noted that "women are the natural teachers and peacemakers".

No longer can our culture withstand the developmental gap between male and female. While competition need not be scorned by either men or women, because it is healthy in many respects, still it must be subsumed within the interpersonally relational context. Women must no longer condone many of the competitive pursuits of their husbands, especially where greed, pollution, and war are concerned. All of these produce more poverty and increased breakdown of society. And ultimately it leaves women without a voice and burdened with the maintenance of family and rearing their children essentially alone—in the midst of the greed, pollution, and wars.

Consequently, women must no longer collude with the immaturity of their male family members, and must demand that every family member reach full maturity. And men must do likewise. I fully realize that there are cooperative, interpersonally relational males—and I have come to know and enjoy several as close friends. There are also competitive females who have chosen to live their lives according to stereotypical "men's rules" and suffer with interpersonal relational difficulties. I am merely referring to the *stereotypes* we observe and have perpetuated in our culture. My research has shown that many men do not reach K-3, nor females go beyond it, due to fear of repercussions from important relationships, in particular the relationships with spouses or other family members. Consequently, co-dependency remains.

Still, the cooperative developmental stage (K-3) is *not* full maturity for either male or female. Only in realizing the development of the full self, through all of the stages Kegan has observed, will any of us experience full maturity. This is a daunting task and it is the most important way that women will truly find their voice and men will become true partners. It is the way in which our culture will be healed.

Summary

We have discussed the research describing the evolutionary adult development for both men and women, which is necessary for the personal and cultural healing of humanity. There is much to ponder in this regard. The time has arrived when men and women need to discover how to become true partners, to overcome their co-dependency, and to develop genuine empathy for one another, in terms of their human differences as well as their similarities. This is the way they can achieve the cooperation and harmony that is rightfully theirs, so that they may live it for the betterment and transformation of humanity.

A false masculinity has justified the character of the corporate world far too long. We have witnessed suicidal militarism and corrupt policies which direct our government, secrecy and exclusion which guide the judgments of the church, and the reduction of humanity to the rationalization of objectivity. In this way we have denied the people of the world the validity of the feminine, of the feelings, in both women and men. In the next chapter we will present the research, coming from many female voices, that has begun to influence the situation for the better.

PART TWO
the New Evolutionary Journey

CHAPTER SIX
Recovering Women's Voices

I have come to believe, from my own research and that of others discussed in the previous chapter that women are at the forefront of major transformational change in our culture. And this is true all over the world, not just in the USA. The *majority* of women in our country, in my view, have been socialized into the *interpersonal* stage 3 described by Kegan's work. Yet the gender co-dependency still remains to a great extent. Still, many women are breaking free of the patriarchal stereotypes and creating an ever widening developmental gap between themselves and their competitive male family members. This poses a distinct threat for their men. What is it precisely that is happening?

This phenomenon is not so prevalent in so-called third world countries, yet it is happening nevertheless. The phenomenon is predominantly associated with more well educated women who make up a sizeable proportion of the female population in our country. The net result is that women are finding the *voices* that they lost or buried during adolescence because of cultural messages. Gilligan's insight into the loss of voice is being verified in many ways today.

Higher education has been opening women's minds to new ideas and to experiences they have ignored or denied because of cultural bias. No longer is it men's thought that is moving them. In finding her own voice, a woman acknowledges her own feminine wisdom and she speaks it *for* herself and *to* others. It is almost as if women are *re-membering* things they subconsciously knew from earlier in their lives. I am convinced that in order for humanity to break free of the hold that the patriarchal system has had in our culture, women must find their own feminine voices so as to take the lead in enabling evolutionary transformation.

On the other hand, there are women coming to the forefront, especially among the very conservative, who have *not* found their own voices, but rather are still parroting the patriarchal values. I have seen this among some women who are campaigning for political office. Other women look up to them believing that they are witnessing someone who knows and understands herself, simply because she is speaking out, and who is capable of making real change. This is usually not the case because of the very *competitive* manner in which these women present themselves. Recently I had a phone conversation with a male friend of my two oldest sons. This fifty-year old man spoke about two women elected in primaries in California to run for the offices of governor and US senator. Both of these women had been successful in the business world. He remarked how "brutal and aggressive" these women had been in their campaigning. I believe that these are *not* women who are actually experiencing their own voices, and that they are *not* in touch with their deeper hidden wisdom at all. Such women are mired in the competitive patriarchal system and feel the need to *act like men* in order to win.

Evolutionary Shifts in Society Today

A number of issues stand out in my own research with women. The findings pertain to several areas of life and involve a complexity of variables. To begin with, there are distinct differences between the childhood/adolescent period in contrast with the adulthood/mid-life years. In my view there is an *innate* evolutionary point that lies between these two periods in our lifespan, designed to bring about a shift toward further development, *if the person chooses it.* To be useful, this evolutionary shift demands that a person turn inward to examine her own feelings, attitudes, and beliefs. Yet no one is conscious of this need until some type of difficulty brings to awareness that there must be a change in the self or lifestyle. This shift is difficult and is accompanied by a considerable amount of guilt for women, due to the necessity of breaking with many traditions previously thought to be secure, sacred, and necessary for receiving love.

From Kegan's point of view, developmental stages are the same for both men and women. Stages shift from preoccupation with self to a focus on relationships with others. (Focus on self at stage 2 shifts to interpersonal focus at stage 3, then again to focus on self at a deeper level in the shift to stage 4. The shift toward stage 5 is once again toward others.) The actual manner in which the shifts from one stage to another are manifest in a person, whether male or female, is severely contaminated by the *messages* from the patriarchal culture. The contamination is precisely due to the stereotypes of what is "ideally" masculine and feminine, and is maintained by the gender co-dependency described in the previous chapter. These messages are accumulated during childhood and adolescence and act as a kind of programming for the life to follow in adulthood. They are initiated in the primary family culture and are reinforced by the larger culture.

Childhood and Adolescent Findings

Messages are mental constructs that repeatedly "broadcast" to the individual *the way things are* for that person, regardless of whether there is any basis in fact. In general, *perception is everything,* especially for young people, and it is very difficult to change a perception when it is strongly believed to be "true." Persons reared in very dysfunctional families have no way to check out the truth or falsity of their messages for many years.

There are a number of ways that messages can be communicated. They may be verbally presented to a child by a parent or teacher, or the child may *assume* the message from her own experience by the way she is treated. The family of origin, and its structure, is the foundation for healthy development in childhood. This is the milieu where evolutionary development is promoted or hindered. It is also the area where the seeds of cultural messages are first sown. For example, parental rejection and neglect are directly related to a negative sense-of-self in a child and extend to a false religious image of God as judging and punishing. A poor or disturbed family structure in which parents are either too lenient or too controlling, or there is domestic violence, divorce, and multiple marriages, does not provide a sense of order and security for a developing child. Conversely, parental warmth and acceptance, and a solid family structure, promote a healthy sense-of-self as well as a more positive image of God. The net result for the child is "I am loveable and God loves me, too."

Many messages will arise in the family environment. The sense-of-self developed early in life lingers into adulthood, and especially if it has been negative, will continue to have adverse effects well into the future and tend to retard the evolutionary process. Other caring persons, such as extended family members, can mitigate to some extent the negative effects of early rejection or neglect. Positive attention and affirmation from these individuals enable the child to experience at least some areas of the early life that may elicit a certain level of healthy self-esteem.

Family traumas or tragedies that occur during childhood allow opportunities for *either* positive or negative messages, depending upon the degree of dysfunction in the family. The traumas of physical, verbal, or sexual abuse are found ordinarily in *very* dysfunctional families, and are part of the negative systemic pattern. Other traumas, notably the tragic death or serious illness of a parent or sibling, can be found in any family structure. Healthy families deal with trauma and tragedy in healthy and loving ways, and teach positive messages about life's difficulties. Because dysfunctional families do not possess the skills to deal well with adversity, their children are usually further traumatized by harsh circumstances and the messages that arise. (See Appendix D for some typical messages.)

Roughly half of the women in my sample viewed their early religious training as very inadequate for helping them face life, for overcoming their difficulties, or for understanding the importance of the Divine in relationship to themselves and others. All of them had evaluated the experience of their religious education *through* the lens of their family experience; the more troubled their family life, the less positive and effective was their religious training generally. Nearly one-third of the sample left their religious practice for some years because of this apparent lack of personal "value," and all but one eventually returned, half of these in mid-life.

Kegan referred to *family religion*[96] as a set of beliefs, rules, and rituals that stem from the family of origin, which may or may not be overlaid with formal religious beliefs, rules, and rituals. Whatever the case, the combination of the two is what forms our early sense of how to live our lives. It is only later in the adult years, primarily mid-life, that the kind of questioning may begin which enables a separation of "family religion" from formal religion, so as to bring both into a consciousness that suits the ongoing development of the individual woman.

Adulthood and Mid-life Findings

The important conclusions stemming from the adult lives of women in my study are related primarily to *changes* that have or have not occurred for them since adolescence. We shall see that a number of the mid-life findings are at variance with those of the earlier period in their lives. This is the time when finding one's voice becomes possible.

In chapter 5, I mentioned the positive effect of the women's movement on my subjects. Vatican Council II in the Catholic Church had an equally profound effect on the women in my study. Both of these historical movements served as sources of new ideas, and these ideas became integrated in regard to helping to bring about changes in the women's religious beliefs. They were able to speak their own "truth" and follow their own consciences rather than strictly adhering to the patriarchal element in doctrine and dogma.

In all likelihood, the greater openness proffered by Vatican Council II not only aided their acceptance of the women's movement philosophy, but enhanced the awareness of women's issues in the Church. This was easier for the *younger* women in the sample (over 40 but under 50), who *grew up* with both the feminist insights and those of the Council. The older women were being challenged to *rethink* their earlier values in the light of these influences.

Because of childhood and adolescent messages, there is a high likelihood that a woman will repeat the pattern of her early life in later years in her marriage, with children, and in other significant relationships. Unless a woman from a very dysfunctional family realizes in late adolescence or young adulthood that something different is possible, it is not likely that she could begin to question what needs to be changed. In a number of cases, a conscious inner struggle, and the *commitment not to repeat* the dysfunctional pattern—or divorce, possibly accompanied by a successful second marriage—could remedy the effects of early life situations in the present and for the future.

The majority of the effects of early life and family are redeemable. The evidence from this study is that *most* of the childhood *themes* no longer apply in adulthood. Put another way, while poor self-assessment is inclined to linger into the adult years, new *perceptions* of those earlier experiences are able to change the way *meaning* is made in the present. New meaning enables new behavior.

Adult crises play an important role in altering the effect of early life messages because they call attention to current difficulties, perhaps heretofore unacknowledged, and warn of negative effects from childhood that may repeat. However, it is necessary for persons experiencing such crises to *rework* or *discard* the negative life messages and poorly functioning coping skills, and to adapt those that have worked well in the past to new circumstances. Even a woman who has been reared in an optimal or adequate family situation is not necessarily guaranteed that she will be able to use her positive childhood messages and coping skills appropriately in adulthood. In fact, several women in my study who had been reared in some of the most dysfunctional households made the greatest evolutionary strides. Again, it is *new meaning* that is required, because it can serve as a means of healing the past. This is a difficult task.

Because women form kinship readily, relationships with other women, who are mutually concerned about common issues, are very likely to lead to new meaning-making. In listening to each other's life stories, women are much more likely to change their childhood ways than if they have struggled alone. An exchange of ideas brings ever deepening insight, and they learn *with* others the art of living in empathic relationships. Kegan's work found that this is one of the ways the shift from stage 3 to stage 4 can be enabled.

Forgiveness is an important and necessary process for letting-go of past hurt and resentment. It is a means of *deconstructing* the past and finding new meaning for the present and future. Forgiveness does not involve forgetting past injury or its cause. Rather, it enables the *release* of resentment and fear that *eat away* at self-esteem and inner peace so as not to prevent more appropriate behaviors that are needed for further evolution. It also sets the stage for the reconciliation of important relationships and the healing and re-construction of family life. Forgiveness is a sure path to love.

In using the Myers-Briggs Type Inventory (MBTI)[97] as part of our study, my colleague and I were not only able to assess the personality type of each woman, we were also able to follow the manner in which each woman's personality changed in an evolutionary way, by comparing her type with the cognitive and meaning-making shifts assessed by the Kegan interview. This proved to be a confirmation that personality development is a result of the integration of the *hidden* aspects of one's personality with those that were initially *preferred* by her type.[98] In other words, the hidden aspects become more and more conscious to the person and more readily available for daily usage as the Kegan development progresses. Thus, the person develops a greater capacity for problem solving and new meaning-making. This evolution of the personality type is correlated with Kegan's stages of the evolving self, and helped my research colleague and I to understand something about the unique ways in which different personality types evolve.

The development of the personality not only provides a fuller sense-of-self, but it also brings with it a more open and trusting relationship with the Divine. The growing recognition of the need for close relationships, forgiveness, and reconciliation have the effect of fostering a desire for a closer affiliation with God, not necessarily with religion as once practiced.

I have found that for those women, who were widowed or deeply disappointed by some of their human relationships, a growing closeness with the Divine allowed them to work through their grief, to transcend their difficulties, and to find inner peace. This was surely an evolutionary shift. These women have learned "that while happy events make life delightful...they do not lead to self-discovery and growth and freedom. That privilege is reserved to the things and persons and situations that cause us pain."[99]

As the women gained a fuller sense of their self-systems (Kegan stage 4 and beyond) they were also more able to engage in fruitful discussion with women and men from other religious traditions, even those that are non-Christian. They seem to be non-threatened by these differences. Many have awakened to the fact that women are not respected as fully adult members of the Catholic Church. There is a sense of being patronized repeatedly. Many had very negative experiences with members of the clergy, who appeared to feel uneasy with ideas and insights coming from mature women. To these women it is evidence that the clergy senses women may be changing the church from the grass roots, and that these men can no longer maintain the privileged position they once assumed.

The foregoing conclusions from my research indicate that the midlife period presents serious challenges for women, which contribute to their further development and an evolution toward ever greater human maturity. These challenges initiate personal growth as well as the possibility of cultural transformation if shared in the wider community. It is important to reiterate that no developmental shift is possible without effort and struggle, sometimes serious psychological pain. For a woman, the movement from an *interpersonal to a personal* focus (K-3 to K-4) requires a break with many cultural dictums regarding appropriate female behavior, as well as wresting free from the gender co-dependency that has kept her feeling trapped for so long. There is much guilt experienced because of this, often a feeling as if she is selfishly depriving her loved ones of love and caring.

For a man, the movement, from a *competitive and achievement-oriented* focus to a *co-operative and collaborative one* (K-2 to K-3), places him in an entirely new type of relationship with others, one that seems threatening and deprived of a privileged position, much as Gilligan had found. He will be forced to rethink the patriarchal norms which have enmeshed him for so long. If his wife is simultaneously shifting into a focus on finding her own voice and her true place in society, it will create a gap in the experience of his home life that can be devastating.

But a question remains. How do these shifts come about? What exactly does a person experience at this time in life? Kegan describes the type of change, the shift from one stage to the next, but he says little about the way this proceeds. In the next section we look at what women experience as they undergo this journey, by considering the inner, personal experience rather than the formal, more abstract findings. This study utilizes the actual *voices* of women to supply the data to discern their *ways* of knowing.

Women's Ways of Knowing

A study was developed by a group of four female psychology professors, working at four separate colleges and universities, to uncover and describe the ways of knowing that women have cultivated and learned to value. Belenky et al [100] had come to believe that these ways of knowing "are powerful but have been neglected and denigrated by the dominant intellectual ethos of our time." This team also wished to describe the multitude of obstacles women must overcome in developing the power of their minds and the recovery of their voices.

To accomplish this they devised a plan to interview women from many walks of life, 135 in all. Analysis of these interviews was challenging because each team member, with her own unique perspective and voice, had to listen carefully to the other team members, as well as to the interviewees, in order to be able to write with a single voice for the sake of the "collective we."

In their book they describe five different perspectives from which women view reality and draw conclusions about knowledge, truth, and authority. Though they were very aware of the work of both Chodorow and Gilligan, and also the other developmental research done at Harvard, the Belenky team decided to proceed not only with a descriptive work, but also with a method of organizing their data into what they referred to as *ways of knowing* and making meaning. During analysis of the interviews, the team became aware that the women revealed five distinct ways of knowing: 1) silence, 2) received knowledge, 3) subjective knowledge, 4) procedural knowledge, and 5) constructed knowledge.

The group recognized:

- that these five ways of knowing are not necessarily fixed, exhaustive, or universal categories,
- that they are abstract or "pure" categories that cannot adequately capture the complexities and uniqueness of an ual woman's thought and life,
- that similar categories can be found in men's thinking, and
- that other researchers might organize their observations differently.

With this fourth statement the team members implied that they were reluctant to refer to these categories as a stage theory. Their analysis adopted a stance of trying to honor each woman's point of view, method of explanation, and standard of evaluation, while simultaneously grouping their responses into categories. [101]

Silence

Silence was the simplest way of knowing the Belenky group was able to discern. Only three women exhibited this category. These silent women were among "the youngest and the most socially, economically, and educationally deprived" of all those interviewed. The team selected the name for this category because the absence of voice in these women was so salient. Figures of speech suggesting gaining a voice were used repeatedly by many of the women to describe how they experienced their own growth and development, particularly the growth of mind. Yet such images were conspicuously absent from the descriptions given by the women of silence.

One theme that stood out with the "silent" women was that words were perceived as weapons, and were used to separate and diminish people, rather than to connect and empower them. There was a constant worry that they would be punished for speaking out.[102] This concurs with the findings in my own study. Negative messages do not have to be given verbally by someone else; they can be assumed from one's experience and imbedded in the conscious or subconscious mind to the detriment of the sense-of-self. These women experienced being seen but never heard and were extremely held bound by the "authority" of the patriarchal system. They were reared in very dysfunctional families.

Received Knowledge

Listening to the voices of others is the dominant theme of the women in this category. While the "silent" women thought of themselves as "deaf and dumb" and were unaware of the power of words to transmit knowledge, the women in this group thought of words as *central* to the knowing process. They frequently referred to "enjoying listening" and experienced it as a very active and demanding process. Yet they often perceived the information given by others as providing "the only right answer" and had little confidence in their ability to share their own thoughts. Moreover, these received knowers were frequently surprised to hear others speaking ideas that were aligned with their own. Still, these women were more apt to think of authorities, rather than friends, as sources of "truth."

According to the Belenky group, received knowers are intolerant of ambiguity. They like predictability and clarity, and want to know exactly what they are expected to do, and what they are responsible for. Most of the women in this group were drawn from social service agencies or were very young students just beginning their college careers. In pluralistic and intellectually challenging environments, this way of thinking quickly disappears. If it does not, the student is likely to drop out or be pushed out early in the process. "Reliance on authority for a single view of the truth is clearly maladaptive for meeting the requirements of a complex, rapidly changing, pluralistic, egalitarian society, and for meeting the requirements of educational institutions, which prepare students for such a world."[103]

Women at the position of received knowledge believe that all knowledge originates outside of self; therefore they look to others for a definition of who they are. Common questions are , "What do they think of me?" and "What would they want me to become?" If one can only see the self as mirrored in the eyes of others, the tendency is great to live up to other's expectations, and to be especially at the mercy of the opinions of authorities. If a person in a powerful position tells such a woman that she is wrong, or bad, or crazy, she believes it. However, if an authority figure seeks out and praises the intelligence of one of these, it may alter her whole way of seeing herself. Thus, conceptions of right and wrong are likely to be as black and white in defining the self as when defining the moral realm.[104] These women are essentially very dualistic.

Subjective Knowledge

Women in this category begin to experience their *inner voice.* They feel with their *gut,* listen to what it says to them, and make decisions according to this subjective, intuitive knowledge. They have "moved from passivity to action, from self as static to a self as becoming, from silence to a protesting inner voice and *infallible* gut." They now possess a new conception of truth, one that is personal, private, and subjectively known or intuited. This subjective knowledge is also dualistic in the sense that there is still the conviction that there are right answers. The source of their knowledge has simply shifted from outer to inner experience. Because truth now resides within the person it can negate those answers supplied by the outside world.

Of all the women in the Belenky study, nearly half were predominately subjectivist in their thinking. They cut across class, ethnic, age and educational boundaries. In a world that emphasizes rationalism and scientific thought, subjectivist women are bound to experience personal and social costs. They are at a special disadvantage when they go about learning and working in a more public setting. Yet, this kind of subjectivism is a type of inner contemplation and understanding that are primary routes to basic knowledge, and even to the realm of Divine Wisdom. (I saw this in my own study among those women whose personality type tested as *intuitive* by the MBTI.)

Subjective knowing holds within it the distinct possibility of leading a woman into a quest for self-knowledge. More than half of the women exhibiting this way of knowing showed a tendency in this direction (roughly half of the total sample). Many began to end unhealthy relationships and to move out on their own. These decisions were accompanied by a broad range of intense emotions, yet the women were determined to take the risks. Some were driven to action by their inner voice and exhibited an almost obsessive preoccupation with a choice between self and other. Their action was on behalf of self as opposed to denying self and living for and through others.

These findings are very descriptive of the evidence I uncovered from women who were experiencing the shift from Kegan stage 3 to stage 4. It represents the beginning of a contemplative way of life, albeit a psychological one, not yet spiritual. These women are experiencing themselves changing, and are going with the flow no matter how difficult.

Procedural Knowledge

Procedural knowing involves the development of the *voice of reason*. In the shift toward self-knowledge the women in this category initially relied on subjective intuition *and* received knowledge. When the women encountered situations in which their old ways of knowing were challenged, they at first experienced an inner conflict, which seemed to be an attempt to stifle their inner voice and draw them back into a world of silent obedience. The tendency was to *defend* their subjectivism.

Gradually they were able to see that it was possible for intuition to deceive, that gut reactions can be irresponsible and no one's gut feeling is infallible. They began to adapt a way of *reasoned reflection* and to understand that they can know things they have never seen or touched before. It is not clear why some of these women made this move while others did not.

Initially this part of the journey was not experienced as progress. The inner voice diminished in volume and seemed to lack authority. It also turned critical and told them that their ideas were stupid. The net result was that the women began to think before they spoke. They initiated a determined effort to acquire and apply procedures for obtaining and communicating knowledge. This proved difficult, even dangerous at times, because women had not developed the various *disciplines* for acquiring knowledge. Until now they had simply accepted the knowledge that had been the domain of men for so long. Yet, on some level, their intuition spurred them onward with the quest for self—the True Self.

Central to the procedural knowledge position is a preoccupation with *ways of looking*. Different people have different opinions, and a right to have them. The women in this category see knowledge as a process, and are interested not merely in what people think, but in *how* they go about forming their opinions and ideas. Those who begin this developmental shift initially feel distressed, because they see no way to get out from behind their own way of looking and enter into another perspective. They need to develop procedures for understanding where others "are coming from" and how to communicate with them. To put one's trust in procedural knowledge requires *talk* to discern the *track* of another's thinking.[105] This is the type of self-knowledge that I observed when a woman is at least Kegan stage 4 or moving beyond.

There is a difference between knowledge and understanding. *Understanding* involves intimacy and equality between self and other. It entails *acceptance* and precludes *evaluation*. Understanding is *connected* knowing. Connected knowers know that other peoples' experiences can only be approximated, so they can gain only limited access to their knowledge. Still, they must act as connected, rather than separate, in order to see the other in her or his terms.

Evaluation, which puts the other at a distance, placing the self above the other, *quantifies* a response to the other that should remain *qualitative*. This is *separate* knowing and we refer to it as *knowledge*. At the heart of separate knowing is *critical thinking*. In a sense, separate knowing is the opposite of subjectivism, and is mostly applied in the scientific realm. However, both connected and separate knowing are needed in all disciplines to some extent. Both varieties of procedural knowledge are "objective" in the sense of being oriented away from the knower's self toward the object the knower seeks to either analyze or understand.

Constructed Knowledge

There are a number of characteristics that are central to women who exemplify this way of knowing. First, they are articulate and reflective people who notice what is happening to others and care about the lives of people around them. Second, they are intensely self-conscious (not self-centered), aware of their own thoughts, judgments, moods, and desires. Third, each is concerned with issues of inclusion and exclusion, separation and connection. Fourth, these women *fight* to find their own voice, their own way of expressing what they know and care about. And fifth, they have learned the profound lesson that even the most ordinary human being is engaged in the construction of knowledge.

"To learn to speak in a unique and authentic voice, women must 'jump outside' the frames and systems authorities provide and create their own frame." In other words, the framework that has been constructed by the patriarchal system in regard to the stereotypical *definition* of femi-nine, must be seriously questioned, even abandoned, in favor of woman's authentic experience. To do this a woman needs to construct her knowl-edge by reclaiming her self through the integration of personally impor-tant, intuitive knowledge with knowledge learned from others. She must weave together the strands of rational and emotive thought and integrate objective and subjective knowing.

It cannot be emphasized enough that the quest for self and voice is central to the transformation of a woman's way of knowing. *Silent* women have little awareness of their intellectual capabilities. They are selfless and voiceless in the presence of others, and assert that *only* external authorities know the truth, and are all powerful.

For women at the *received* and *procedural* knowledge positions other voices and external truths dominate. The sense of self is embedded either in external definitions and roles or in identifications with institu-tions, disciplines, and methods. This typically means a tendency toward adherence to sex-role stereotypes or second-rate status as a woman in a man's world. At the position of *subjective* knowledge, the quest for self, or protection of a space for growth of self, is of primary importance. This often means a turning away from others and a denial of external authority. [106]

"It is in the process of sorting out the pieces of the self and of searching for a unique and authentic voice that women come to the basic insights of constructivist thought: *All knowledge is constructed,* and *the knower is an intimate part of the known.*" Women arrive at these two insights in their search for a core self that responds to shifts in situa-tion and context. The answers to all questions vary depending upon the context in which the question is asked and on the frame of reference of the person doing the asking. As women share these among themselves, a transformation in understanding of self begins to generalize and affect how women think about truth, knowledge, and expertise. In recog-nizing that all knowledge is a construction and that truth is a matter of the context in which it is embedded, a woman can greatly expand the possibilities of how she can think about anything, even those most elementary and obvious things. [107]

Simply because the Belenky team has described the five ways of knowing in the order indicated does not imply that they occur in that order for a particular woman. This is dependant upon other factors, particularly personality type (MBTI). Intuitive types evolve in a different manner from sensate types, just as thinkers differ from feelers, because the perception of their life experience differs. Thus, the authors suggest that they prefer not to consider their approach a stage theory. What is certain is that the earlier ways of knowing must be integrated and evolutionary trajectory has been followed.

The Healing Connection

As a confirmation of elements of my own research I offer the following discussion. Jean Baker Miller and Irene Stiver[108] spent many years, at the Women's Center at Wellesley College, studying how women's relationships are formed and the way they heal. They had formed a group with two other colleagues, Judith Jordan and Janet Surrey. All of them were clinicians with many years experience, and had come to recognize that traditional psychodynamic theories and forms of practice neglected or misunderstood many aspects of women's experience. Their aim was to try to understand women's psychological development, the problems women encounter, and what to do about them.

The Wellesley group's theory emerged out of the exchanges that occurred between them, from the flow of their interaction. Individual ideas became enlarged and transformed in the interchange. Thus, what arose was not what it was when the discussion began and a joint creation came about. They confronted the notion of separation, which was thought to be the goal by which we should define ourselves as healthy human beings. Their experience led them to a different emphasis for understanding psychological development, one that is about connection between people, about how we create them, and how disconnections derail them throughout our lives.[109]

Connections

What the four team members came to see as women's valid close connections to others were frequently dismissed as "masochistic," "dependent," or "engulfing" by a mental health profession dominated by male views of development. Signs of psychological health were deemed to be independence, controlled emotional expression, and separation, particularly from one's mother. Gradually, the group discussions enabled the four of them to be more confident with challenging traditional psychological assessments of the women they encountered. They were moving away from many basic assumptions of both professional and popular "wisdom."

What my own research had taught me was that women's propensity for connection was the very necessary factor that created and maintained kinship in both families and among friends. The Wellesley group also came to understand that connection not only contributed significantly to women's growth and development, it was precisely what enabled women to heal. For too long, this basic human activity has not been well recognized or described in ways that portray its importance, complexity, and creativity. But connection is an activity that is going on all the time, nonetheless.

When we speak of participating in others' psychological development, we are referring to a form of activity that is essential to human life. As we have already mentioned, our society has assigned this fundamental activity, and its distinctive wisdom, to women. The new perspective on connection presents a vision of psychological and emotional health for *all people,* male and female alike. This new vision of mutual development includes not only individuals and families, but also workplaces, schools, and other institutions—all of life.

The Wellesley group does not intend to falsely idealize women, or to imply that the knowledge and wisdom of how to create and sustain growth-fostering relationships is limited by gender, nor do I. Individual women can be coercive, destructive, or abusive in some of the worst aspects of power-over relationships with others. But it is a general fact that in our culture, as well as worldwide, it is the women who have done most of the work of building the developmental aspects of relationships for society as a whole. It is therefore our belief that it is from women's lives and experience that we can best learn about the potential power of a relational approach toward all of human development.[110]

Disconnections

A disconnection is the psychological experience of rupture that occurs whenever a child or adult is prevented from participating in a mutually empathic and mutually empowering interaction. Disconnections can be minor; they inevitably occur all through childhood and adulthood. They can also resolve into reconnection—a better connection. Two key features usually prove to be necessary for a reconnection to take place:

- One must be able to take some action within the relationship to make one's experience known.
- The other people in the relationship must be able to respond in a way that leads toward a new and better connection.

All of us, to varying degrees, find it difficult to talk about our behavior with the people we have hurt or let down. Some people may also be unaware of how they affect others and have a hard time allowing other people to tell them. In any relationship where one person has more power, the danger of harm increases. It is much harder for the less powerful person to alter the course of an interaction.

Those people who bring about the most serious disconnections and violations of others will also have the most trouble engaging in growth-enhancing interactions about their own behavior. [111]

Consider the power element in parent-child relationships. If a parent and child are able to discuss their disconnections in a caring way, even if agreement cannot be reached, there are two things that can be learned. First, the child will learn that from time to time she will experience difficult feelings with others. But most important, she will feel an increase in her ability to have an effect on her relationships, to see that she does have an impact. Second, her parents will learn too, because most of the time they will feel good when they are able to understand their child's experience and respond to it well.

Interactions that can lead to serious disconnection may be experienced in a number of ways. Disconnections, that may not be noticeable, can occur in multiple daily interactions over a long period of time. Others may arise in more gross and obviously destructive situations. Repetition of one or more of these kinds of interactions is chronic in very dysfunctional families, and can lead to serious psychological problems. The longterm consequences of these disconnections are most serious for children because this is where implied messages are conceived as well as *internal* relationship patterns. Children construct these messages and relational patterns because they are the least powerful members in a relationship. Still, while sadness, anger, and fear are difficult feelings, they can be borne best in connection with *other* people, such as extended family members, who can engage with them.

The Wellesley group came to recognize that there is a *central relational paradox* that is observed in disconnected relationships. The child or adult continues to *seek connections* but learns that she can only do so by keeping more and more of her experience, and her reactions to her experience, out of these connections. The Wellesley group believes that this phenomenon is basic to understanding many psychological problems and the therapy needed for these problems.[112] Thus, disconnected relationships cannot possibly contribute to a woman's sense-of-self or be a help in finding her own voice. In many cases only a suitable therapeutic relationship can provide the needed connection for healing and growth.

Summary

We have discussed three distinct studies, with unique foci, that illustrate the direction of growth and healing a woman needs to explore in order to reach the level of development necessary for discovering her True Self and becoming a challenge to our society for cultural healing. In the next chapter we shall consider the progress already being made in a variety of situations and the manner in which it can continue to heal.

CHAPTER SEVEN

Women's Role in Human Evolution Today

The problems we have today, as brutal, ravaging, and regrettable as they are, in fact are an opportunity. They represent the chaos necessary to produce an evolutionary shift in human consciousness, a spiritual transformation in human behavior, and healing of our cultures. Women are at the forefront of this shift worldwide, and some men are contributing to their effort. As women are developing in consciousness they are finding their voices which many in the third world never knew they possessed. And those men who are influenced by them are able to support and help activate their efforts.

In this chapter I want to describe some of the accomplishments women are achieving in many parts of the world, but I also want to point out the societal stumbling blocks they face as well. The previous chapter described how women are changing. Now we shall examine the outcomes of these changes for the women as well as for humanity at large. The only way this shift can happen is for women to implement an irreversible effect on the co-dependency problem that stems from the patriarchal system.

Patriarchal Stumbling Blocks

Media Images in America

A few years ago I viewed an educational film at the Wellesley Center for Women, co-directed by a young man who was, at the time, among only a handful of men who have majored in women's studies in college.

Jackson Katz,[113] as a result of his understanding of the issues, has a rare gift for presenting feminist insights regarding gender and power. He is capable of approaching men in such a way that helps them think critically without becoming defensive, at the same time offering women valuable new perspectives into masculinity.

Katz argues in "Tough Guise" that there is a crisis in masculinity that offers *guises* for men that come loaded with attendant dangers for women. The film is referenced to American culture today and the media that subtly portray the problems. It looks at masculinity in a new way, "not as a fixed, inevitable, natural state of being, but rather as a projection, a performance, a mask that men often wear to shield their vulnerability and hide their humanity." These images tell *part* of the story about changes occurring in American men over the last generation.

The baby boomer generation has been credited with catalyzing and renewing the women's movement, one of the key transformative social movements in the history of the human race. Those who have been born in the last quarter of the 20th century have not simply reacted to this social change, they have literally grown up with it. Many young men, of all races and ethnicities, have embraced new notions of sexual equality, and are *seeking* relationships with women as friends, lovers and husbands, classmates, colleagues, and fellow workers.

Yet many other men have reacted very poorly to these challenges—and it's not just those living in extreme situations like the Taliban in Afghanistan, Al Qaeda, or tribal areas in Africa or elsewhere. Many of these men, in particular those coming from very conservative right wing and fundamentalist religious groups, have had their long-standing images of manhood threatened by women's increased assertions of strength, integrity, and social and economic power. These perceived threats have manifested as a backlash resulting in increased violence against women and girls in spite of decades of feminist anti-violent activism.

Katz sees that the images of masculine and feminine produced by the media for TV, video games, billboards, and films, *produce us* as well. We tend to become what we pay attention to; we are programmed by these media. It is one more way of receiving messages that we will need to reexamine. Though feminists have tended to analyze these images with a focus on women, Katz has focused on the ways these images portray men. Young men in the past few decades have been challenged by women in areas never considered by earlier generations. Even so, there is one area where men as a group still assume to have a significant advantage over women as a group. That is in the areas of physical size and strength, which for many men have become increasingly important for proving manhood.

At the same time, women's bodies are portrayed by the media and the fashion world as thinner, more waif-like and younger than bodies of women in the real world. Katz notes that showing women in this way symbolically takes power away from them because they literally take up less space in our world and thus are less threatening. So for young men who have experienced considerable change due to the women's movement, keeping up the posturing is still very evident. These men live with one foot in the egalitarian world with women, while the other foot remains in the patriarchal world. All of this causes me to question if the rapid increase in female obesity is somehow correlated with the media images, possibly as a subconscious backlash.

Katz points out that "tough guy posing, even though it's often just an act, also has the effect of *keeping men in line"* from a patriarchal standpoint. Millions of boys and men learn early in life that a *real man* is a stoic individualist, which means "you don't complain, don't admit weakness, and don't ever let anyone see your anxiety." This sort of conditioning starts very young, and is necessary for maintaining the competitive stance that proves they are *manly* men (Kegan stage 2). It also prevents them from becoming sympathetic human beings, attentive to other's needs, and unresponsive to anything beyond competition and "power over." This conditioning reflects what Gilligan had noted about boys losing their voices by age four.[114] The pretense of omnipotence and invulnerability is not just emotionally damaging, it also gets a lot of men killed—in gangs, war, and other violent endeavors. These tough images not only affect poor black men, as well as poor working-class white men, they also have an impact on white suburban, middle-class males.

In the past 25 years, there has been increased scholarship in the field of masculinity and how men have *not* adjusted to the changes catalyzed by the women's movement. This work has accelerated the feminist project of shedding light on the intimate details of men's lives, in hope that this understanding can be influential in breaking down sexual inequality and improving the lives of both women and men. Furthering our understanding of the ways that media imagery influences the construction of masculinity is a critical part of this effort.[115]

Third World Women's Issues

Patriarchal dominance is relatively mild and subtle in America in the lives of most women, with the exception of the right wing fundamentalist groups, the militias, and the trafficking of women into sweat shops and prostitution that remains mostly underground in the US. But it is a very different story in Asia, the Middle East, and Africa. Because poverty is so rampant, young girls are frequently sold by their parents into prostitution or sweat shops, forms of outright slavery. In other instances girls are abducted or falsely promised jobs as housemaids or salesgirls, only to be sold into prostitution.

Nicholas Kristof and his wife Sheryl WuDunn,[116] journalists from the New York Times, spent several years visiting Asian, Muslim, and African nations and documenting the conditions in which poor, rural women live. They interviewed women who had been victims of the cultural crimes of prostitution and other forms of slavery. From these women's stories the Kristofs gained the insight that *women aren't the problem but the solution. The plight of girls is no more a tragedy than an opportunity.*[117] They found mounting evidence that helping women can also be a successful poverty-fighting strategy anywhere in the world.

The Kristofs' agenda focused on three particular categories of abuse inflicted on the women of the world: sex trafficking and forced prostitution; gender based violence, including honor killings and mass rape; and maternal mortality including genital cutting. Their hope is to recruit westerners to join the movement to emancipate women and fight global poverty by unlocking women's power as economic and moral catalysts. This is my hope as well.

The abuses encountered by the authors are viewed as criminal in the western world. While these issues have been known for years, concerns about terrorism after the 9/11 attacks triggered a new interest in them by the military and counterterrorism agencies. It has been found that the countries that nurture terrorism are disproportionately those where women are marginalized. The reason there are so many Muslim terrorists has little to do with the Koran, but a great deal to do with the lack of robust female participation in the economy and society in many Islamic countries. Similarly, prostitution and other forms of female slavery found in Thailand, Cambodia, India, and China continue to exist because of no strong female voices in opposition. Genital cutting is rampant in Africa where women believe it to be a necessary part of their culture. Poverty and lack of education underlie all of these conditions.

According to the Kristofs, India almost certainly has more girls and women *enslaved* in brothels than any other country. Those who start out enslaved often accept their fate eventually and sell sex willingly, because they know nothing else and are often too stigmatized to hold other jobs. Though China has by far more prostitutes than India, fewer of them are forced into brothels against their will. Actually, China has few brothels because many of the prostitutes are free-lancers. It is the countries with the most straight-laced and conservative sexual standards, such as India, Pakistan, and Iran, that have disproportionately large numbers of forced prostitutes. [118]

The forced prostitutes in these countries are kept tightly guarded and, in many cases, naked to prevent escape. Furthermore, most brothels are managed by women who beat the girls frequently and viciously when they refuse to cooperate or appear to "get out of line" by protesting the way they are treated. Drugs, especially methamphetamines are given to the girls to keep them compliant so that many become addicted to "meth", and because of this addiction refuse to leave the brothels or return later after they have been rescued. Usually the girls are not allowed to use condoms, so that many live short lives, dying of AIDs by their late twenties.

If a girl should become pregnant, the baby is frequently taken away at birth and kept in the brothel to become a future prostitute. Even boys are used as prostitutes when they become older. These children are frequently beaten and starved. It is estimated that there are at least 3 million women and girls (and a small number of boys) worldwide who can be termed enslaved in the sex trade. These are people who are literally the property of another person and who could be killed by their owner without cause.

While there has been progress in addressing many humanitarian problems in the last few decades, sex slavery has actually worsened due to the collapse of Communism in Eastern Europe and Indochina. Because of economic distress criminal gangs have arisen and filled the power vacuum, creating new markets for female flesh in Cambodia.

Thailand, and India.[119]

One of the worst blocks to helping women and girls is the total lack of government or local police support. Often if a girl escapes her brothel and reports to the police she will be sent back from where she came, sold into a new brothel, or raped by the police. The usual attitude is that prostitution is inevitable. These poor girls are sacrificed to "keep harmony in society" so that "good girls can be safe," as if poor girls couldn't also be good girls. In general, the government does not support them because of fear of being discovered and reported to the rest of the world. The tools to crush modern slavery exist, but the political will is lacking.[120]

Rape has become endemic in Africa. Besides being used as a weapon of war, it is frequently used to force an unwilling girl into marriage. If a young man is too poor to afford a bride price (a man's dowry) or he thinks her family will not accept him, he may arrange with several friends to kidnap the girl and then rape her. That immediately improves his bargaining position, because she is ruined and will have difficulty marrying anyone else. The rapist is never prosecuted by law. Women who run for political office must be protected by security forces because of the possibility of being raped by opposition party gangs. [121]

The cult of virginity has been extremely widespread for thousands of years going back at least as far as the Hebrew Bible, as well as in Greece, and China, and elsewhere. It is considered a small matter for a woman to starve to death, but for her to lose her chastity is a calamity. This harsh view is no longer prevalent in most of the world, with the exception of the Middle East. Yet, often the simplest way to punish a rival family is to violate their daughter. Because she was violated, or for committing fornication, her father or some other male family member is duty bound to kill her. Even in the case that a girl has fallen in love with a man, though there may be no proof that they have had sex, her family is likely to perform an "honor killing." Autopsies of victims of honor killings frequently reveal the daughter's hymen to be still intact.

Genital cutting, often referred to as female circumcision, has been a common practice in Africa for centuries. Considered a rite of passage for girls, its sole purpose is to inhibit female sexual pleasure, because it is believed the girls will be less likely to seek out sexual liaisons before marriage. Mothers and other family females will perform these procedures on their daughters, and daughters usually want it to be done to them. It frequently results in serious infections because the procedure is initiated with knives or razor blades which have not been cleansed.

Female mortality is high because the women do not have access to medical care, due to poverty and unavailability of services. Especially in difficult deliveries, the mothers suffer damage to the genital area as well as to puncture of the bowel and/or bladder. This causes chronic infection that renders many women as outcasts. In general, male children are given medical attention and vaccination, whereas it is usually denied to females because they are considered less important. Girls are often poorly fed, even to the point of starvation. Infanticide of girl babies is still practiced in various parts of the world even though it has largely been outlawed, but not enforced.

Militarism, *and the patriarchy it defends,* are based on the notion of *power over,* and place women at particular risk for victimization, violation and harm. Civilian casualties now make up as much as 70% of the total casualties of any military action, and women and children make up the majority of civilian casualties.

Military conflict makes women particularly vulnerable because of:

- A breakdown in government and law enforcement,
- Loss of home, separation from family, especially men who may have provided protection, and becoming refugees,
- Loss of jobs and income,
- Rape, sexual slavery, and trafficking,
- Forced marriages and pregnancies
- Femicide

Violence against women does not end when the fighting ends. Rapes have been committed by UN peace keepers and soldiers who come home and assault there wives. Thousands and thousands of rapes have been committed in recent years in Sierra Leone, Bosnia, Darfur, Rwanda and other countries. The connection between militarism and violence against women is a global issue. Militarism has become *the other terrorism*.[122]

What is Being Accomplished

There is ample evidence that the conditions described above are changing, yet it is anything but an easy task. Western governments, Non-Governmental Organizations (NGOs), private individuals and foundations are cooperating to find ways to end these atrocities. But perhaps the most important element for change is what women are becoming and doing to overcome these conditions. We shall look at three areas that are succeeding in various parts of the globe.

Combating Human Trafficking—Governments and NGOs

Human trafficking is a global industry, not just in third world countries. Within the Western Hemisphere it is an important issue that shapes the relationship between Latin American countries and the United States.[123] Both the United Nations and the United States have developed methods for ranking countries in regard to human trafficking. A ranking score has been allocated to the U.S. as well as 177 other countries. The trafficking of children, especially, is an immensely serious problem that regional governments paired with NGOs must address.

The UN and the U.S. have both provided definitions of trafficking. The U.S. government allows foreign aid partly based on the grade a country receives in its rank on the trafficking scale. Consequently, many regional governments choose to adhere to the U.S. definition rather than the one given by the United Nations. The U.S. State Department is in charge of the trafficking report annually, discusses each country, elaborating on improvements or regression, and gives each a grade.

Illegal immigrants who travel up from Mexico and Central America are especially vulnerable to becoming victims of human trafficking. Though 40% of the trafficking victims in the U.S. come from Latin America, it is not always about migration. One former ambassador to the State Department's program has said "the heart of human trafficking lies in exploitation." And it is every bit as much for labor as for sexual exploitation.

Haiti has a long history of economic destitution. Even before the recent earthquake, 70% of the population in Port-au-Prince was living in poverty, so that the distress of the quake only exacerbated the trafficking problem. Since poverty is the driving force it is likely to take decades to eliminate trafficking if this is the only effort put forth. A moral imperative must be present as well as the maintenance of a political system since the rule of law is lacking there. Haiti has no laws to protect the trafficking of children either as sex slaves or indentured servants who work from morning to night with no pay.

Because of the corruption among law enforcement officials, it is crucial that the U.S. step up its aid to assist victims, not only in Haiti, but throughout the region of Latin America. Assisting NGOs financially can help build the capacity to decrease human trafficking, because these organizations can operate outside the corrupt government and law enforcement systems. Also, U.S. assistance to NGOs can put pressure on the various governments to cooperate in reducing poverty as well as human trafficking.

Foundations and Private Individuals

Cambodia

One example that has proved extremely helpful for young girls in Cambodia involves the intervention of the prestigious, private Overlake School in Redmond, Washington.[124] The principal was looking for a way to teach his very advantaged students about the manner in which most of the people in the world actually live. He contacted a man who believed that keeping girls in school was the way to save them from being trafficked. This man had established an American Assistance program in Cambodia. With the aid of the World Bank and the Asian Development Bank, he was establishing schools in Cambodian villages.

The principal of Overlake School approached the students to sponsor a school in Cambodia as a means of teaching the students about the importance of public service. Though the initial response from both students and parents was mild, the attacks of 9/11 created a more intense interest in which they became much more concerned about the world at large. The students conducted bake sales, car washes and talent shows to raise money, and began to study about the people, culture and history of Cambodia's war and genocide.

They began to build a school on the border of Cambodia and Thailand, an area that is notorious for cheap brothels that cater to Thai men. The school was completed in 2003, and a group of students went to Cambodia to see what they had accomplished. They took boxes of school supplies with them. The sign over the school read "Overlake School" in English as well as the Khmer script of Cambodia. The Americans soon funded an English teacher and arranged for an Internet connection for the school. Cambodian students regularly send e-mails to the American students. This enterprise proved so successful that the Overlake students decided to assist a school in Ghana. Some of the Overlake students have decided on careers to empower people around the world.

Ethiopia

A situation emerged around the problem of widespread rape in Ethiopia. Indignant Americans, mostly women, wrote angry letters demanding change in regard to the legal code that had refused to punish rape in Ethiopia. The Americans also provided financial support and stipends to help one activist woman to pursue her education in Addis Ababa, the Ethiopian capital. These letter writers were mobilized by Equality Now, an advocacy organization founded in 1992 by a woman based in New York.

Funding initially was an uphill struggle for her, but today she has strong support from a number of celebrity women in the U.S. Equality Now has a staff of fifteen in New York, London, and Nairobi, and an annual budget of $2 million. The army of letter writers put pressure on the Ethiopian government to the extent that it was shamed into changing its laws. Today, a man is liable for rape even if the victim later agrees to marry him.[125]

Empowering Native Women Worldwide

There are many women accomplishing amazing things worldwide these days. But the struggle is a difficult one and life-threatening at times. It is dangerous for foreigners to urge local girls to take undo risks. By protesting and running away from brothels women often risk being severely beaten, tortured, or even killed. It is essential to help young women *find their voices.* Through education and empowerment training, girls especially learn that femininity does not entail docility, and that they can nurture assertiveness to allow them to stand for themselves.

This is exactly what has happened in a slum in central India. The inhabitants of this slum are Dalits—Untouchables. They live in shacks on dirty lanes which flow with mud and sewage whenever it rains. Because of the caste system these people have nowhere else to live. One young woman, Usha, thrived despite the odds. Her father is a high-school graduate, and her mother has a ninth-grade education. Because both parents were determined that their children get a solid education, they lived frugally, saving their money to accomplish this. In a slum where no one had ever gone to college, they accomplished something heroic, in that all five of their children, including Usha, graduated from the university.

After Usha graduated with a degree in hotel management, she went back to her village for a visit. She found that the area was overrun with a gang of hoodlums, who had taken control of her village, and were robbing, murdering, and torturing the inhabitants. The Indian authorities did nothing to intervene—a common situation in India—because the people were Untouchables. There was a constant threat of rape to terrorize anyone who dared to speak up against the gang. The more barbaric the behavior, the more the population was forced into acquiescence. Often the people went to the police, and then the police arrested them. Worse still, if a woman complained of being gang raped, the police often gang raped her as well.

On one occasion the gang leader and some of his men came to Usha's family home to threaten her because she had made a complaint against him. He threatened to rape her, throw acid in her face, or murder her if he ever caught her. When he tried to break down the door Usha turned on the gas used for cooking and threatened to throw a lighted match into the house if he broke through the door. The gang leader and his men, upon smelling the gas, backed off. Usha's neighbors gathered in the village, and when they saw how she had forced the gang to retreat, they also gained courage. Some one hundred angry Dalits marched through the village, throwing stones at the gang. Then they went down the street and burned the leader's house to the ground.

Sometime later, because the leader's actions were continuing to threaten the people, the police arrested him for his own safety's sake. When a bail hearing was announced for the leader, hundreds of women from the village marched to the court room. The leader, accompanied by two policemen, mocked and threatened the women, who began to throw chili powder at the three men in order to blind them. When the leader began to plead for mercy from the angry women, they rushed toward him, each woman stabbing him once. His dead body was carried away.

It was obvious that the incident was well planned and that Usha was behind it, even though she was not present. She was arrested and imprisoned for two weeks, but a retired high court judge took her side. The village women gathered together and decided to confess that *all of them* had killed the leader, realizing that the police would have to arrest them all. The frustrated police released Usha, on the condition that she remain in the area.

She began to use her management skills, and started a new life as a community organizer to bring the Dalits together to make pickles, clothing, and other products to sell in the market. She encourages the people to start businesses to improve their incomes so that they can afford more education. Usha's story illustrates the power of a woman to motivate other women *and* men.[126]

Women throughout the Muslim world, India, and Africa are motivating other women to change. When one woman finds her voice, she can help others to do likewise. Women are rescuing other women and girls from brothels, training them to make crafts, bind books, and teaching skills like welding and carpentry. However, because of the poverty, there is a continuing need for financial aid from the Western world.

Kyrgystan

In June, 2010, over a period of three days, more than 2,000 people were killed and hundreds of thousands of people displaced in southern Kyrgystan. The violence erupted between the Uzbek and Kyrgyz. Homes and businesses in Uzbek neighborhoods were burned forcing over 100,000 ethnic Uzbeks to seek refuge by crossing the border into Uzbekistan. Thousands of Uzbeks were left homeless and living in fear. Most observers of this ethnic conflict point to the April, 2010 elections in Kyrgystan where a change in political power sparked the unrest.

The ethnic tensions had been fueled by neglect. Years of unaddressed mistrust and separation among ethnic groups, as well as crumbling social infrastructure and welfare systems, began after the disintegration of the Soviet Union. Two significant trends emerged across the region. The rise in nationalism, which grew in order to create a national identity, had been suppressed under Communism. Also, the gradual erosion of the welfare state as each country attempted to adopt free-market capitalism, together with the nationalism trend, together created a volatile climate where blaming the *other* has been easier than addressing these systemic causes. Then both ethnic groups began purchasing guns to secure themselves and their families.

Women of both ethnic groups were raped and murdered during the unrest in southern Kyrgystan, due to the deep patriarchal culture that permeates the region. Consequently, gender-based violence has not received widespread attention. However, though there are no women in government office, ninety percent of the NGOs are managed by women. When violence broke out in June, women's rights groups were among the first responders to the crisis. Women's crisis centers responded with emergency medical and psychological support for the victims whether they were Uzbek or Kyrgyz women.

Since the 1990s, Kyrgystan has developed one of the most vibrant women's movements in all of Central Asia. Consequently, women's leaders from around the country put forth a strategy for their response over the next five months, including immediate support for women who have experienced violence, documentation of sexual violence, and peace-building efforts among ethnic Uzbek and Kyrgyz women in rural communities throughout Kyrgystan. Women are coming together for common action, reaching out to the most marginalized women, such as sex workers and women living with HIV. In this way, populations often overlooked by general humanitarian efforts, receive aid, support, and safety from additional violence. As the provisional government struggles to determine the future of Kyrgystan, these women will be implementing local peace-building programs and bringing *women's solutions* to national discussions.

It is obvious that investment in the long-term stability in southern Kyrgystan is desperately needed to prevent further repetition of the violence in the future. The Global Fund for Women knows from 23 years of experience in supporting women's initiatives, that the native women best understand the problems in their communities, and are uniquely positioned to implement realistic and effective solutions.[127]

Haiti

Since the fall of the Duvalier dictatorship in 1986, Haitian women have become increasingly more vocal and active in social, political, and economic issues. Their progress in changing gender relations of power within the home, social movements, and the nation has been steady, though not easy. In a country where 45% of men and 49% of women are illiterate, and poverty is endemic, women's organizations have become key to these advances. One network that is helping women gain a voice, literally, is the Haitian Women's Community Radio Network.

The importance of radio and the significance of women taking the microphone cannot be overstated, especially in a country where aggressive patriarchy in the home and society, as well as violence from male partners and the state, have tried to keep them silent. The radio network was founded in 2001, and includes 25 member stations in nine of Haiti's 10 geographic departments. It has trained about 150 women as journalists, program hosts, and production technicians.

The network helps women in various radio stations create programs about local issues, while also producing national-level shows which are aired on member stations. Special one hour programs are produced each month on gender-related topics such as women's political advocacy, gender relations, Haitian women's social realities, violence, HIV-AIDs, and news about women from around the world. They also produce special programs especially for girls ages 11-15 to be used in community schools that instruct girls about their bodies and health issues, as well as relationships between girls and boys.

The network's office and all of its archives, materials, and supplies were destroyed in the January 12, 2010 earthquake. They lost computers, records, cameras, and office furniture. Consequently, the group's work has had to be on hold as the staff reestablishes itself. When they resume their programs their focus will be on the status of women in the catastrophe phase and the participation of women in the reconstruction.

When the network was first initiated, the machismo from men prevented them from accepting women's voices in such an outstanding way. Now they have women who are directors of radio stations, though there are still no women owners. Men are starting to understand, and gender issues are giving way to other radio programs. Yet the women do not want to go backwards, because the relations between men and women are fragile due to the displacement and human loss caused by the earthquake.

Because of the catastrophe following the earthquake, a new form of participation has emerged, where women can be a part of everything. They participate in the big debates about reconstruction, and in planning national development for a new Haiti. The hope is that a process will emerge where women and men can work together to build a new country, and men will no longer be the lone decision makers for everyone. The Haitians do not want the kind of international "help" that they have seen so far, because much of it is about domination. In the context of Haiti's reality today, solidarity is very much needed.[128]

Brazil

Ilda, a 61 year-old female indigenous farmer in Brazil, has been part of the movement for social and economic justice since she was 18. Her parents lost their plot of rural land in the 1960s when the landowner expelled them. She was young and decided to go to Sao Paulo to earn money to help her father buy land. She was unsuccessful. But because she was raised Catholic, and religion was a strong presence in her life, she began to organize people with similar problems through her church in Sao Paulo. She began with a fight for affordable rent, then she started an initiative for lower utility prices and better living conditions. Next she became involved in a movement for housing in Sao Paulo, for the homeless and those living in the *favelas,* the slums.

Ilda's life agenda had changed. Becoming involved in these projects proved to be a great joy for her, in spite of the fact that it was during the time of the Brazilian dictatorship and they could not hold meetings. She, and the families with which she worked, spread a new consciousness to help people learn to liberate themselves. They suffered mistreatment because of this, and were evicted from the houses they rented time and time again. They continued to hope that many good things were ahead of them.

Ilda had married, given birth to five children, and even though they were young, she taught them to be activists like herself. She took a night-time job as a metalworker to earn money to feed her children. Eventually she discovered the Movement of Landless Rural Workers, and began to organize to collect food, clothing, and medicines to take to the country-side. As Ilda became integrated with the movement her dream to return to the countryside became a reality. But after 18 years of marriage she and her husband separated because he disagreed with her involvement in the movement.

Ilda recognizes that women do not recognize their power and strength as women. She says, "When a mother gains her consciousness, she…struggles with all of her heart to guarantee that her children and her children's friends accompany her. And with that, the family is able to mobilize the people to struggle for a better life." She is proud to be a woman and to see other women struggling because she knows therein lies the future. She also works the land with her children.

The Movement of Landless Rural Workers of Brazil is a beacon that represents a burgeoning movement around the world in other countries. They train youth, women, and families to produce food without the use of toxic chemicals. Forest and water preservation are critical for the movement. And producing their own seeds so as to eliminate dependency upon multi-national companies is also important. They produce their own milk because they want to return to their "own womb of production." They have formed cooperatives so that they can operate with *solidarity exchanges.*[129]

The Philippines

Mary Ann Manahan, a woman working in Manila, Philippines, has described how inspiring it has been for her that many young feminists and young activists, in the midst of globalization, are using collective action to build the strength of the most vulnerable women. These are people who have been victims of decades of being battered by wrong agricultural policies and husbands, and in general not being taken care of. She refers to women as *shock absorbers* because they are the first to feel the crises caused by the economic and social insecurity of globalization, and also of the worldwide financial crisis. Women, not only in the Philippines but around the world are bonded by the same ideals and vision: They need to get out of poverty and are doing it through concerted political action. As they are strengthening their economies at a local level, they are also trying to claim their stake in the government.[130]

The Institute of Formation and Religious Studies is located on a narrow street in a very poor neighborhood in Quezon City, Philippines.[131] For more than 40 years it has been developing church leaders, mostly women religious, while teaching personal empowerment and feminist thought. The quality of the education is first-rate, deals with a wide range of pastoral and scholarly church matters, and now attracts students from throughout Asia.

Originally, the institute's courses were based on the Jesuit curriculum for seminarians. But over time, as the voices and positions of religious women grew in the Philippines, paralleling a growth of the women's movement in the United States, the sisters took control of the institute and its curriculum. The programs and courses began to reflect and respond to the changing character of the post-Vatican II church. The institute developed courses that were tied to the social and economic problems that plagued the Philippines, and began programs that would allow students to live with, and immerse themselves in, the conditions of those they were called to serve.

As the institute grew, its leaders began to realize that more formal training in religious studies and theology was necessary to fully prepare future women religious leaders. It developed a two-track curriculum that was intended to meet specific pastoral needs, as well as offering one- or two-year degrees in religious studies and theology. Today the institute offers both undergraduate and master's degrees, and now accepts men in addition to women students. Since the 1990s Catholic students have also been coming from China, Myanmar (Burma) and Vietnam.

India

"Women bring knowledge and a different focus to the table...Until their ideas are fully integrated in planning and development, be it social, or economic or ecclesial, the human family is only walking on one leg." There is no going back. Asian women religious are adding their voices to those of others who are not taking "no" for an answer. They are empowered and empowering other women. [132]

Goa, in southern India, was once a place where pious and obedient nuns came to escape the world, vowing their silence. The convent of St. Monica, a 450 year old cloistered Augustinian foundation, today is a hotbed of feminist theology and one of South Asia's foremost centers of graduate education for religious women. The current leader of this establishment, known as Institute Mater Dei, believes that religious women must no longer serve as handmaids to priests. Because of Vatican II, religious life demands an entirely new and courageous initiative.

The young sisters who attend classes there represent 28 different communities of religious women. They are encouraged and even prodded to speak up forcefully and act boldly, in order to serve God's people more effectively in their various ministries, and just as importantly, to redress India's male-dominated culture in secular society and the church. Currently, they are beginning a three-year degree-granting program at the Pontifical Institute of Philosophy and Religion in Pune, India.

The philosophy of Institute Mater Dei does not focus on the "hot-button" issues of the West, such as the ordination of women, but rather focuses on bringing women into their rightful place in the church. The intent is to help these women return to their ministries with new knowledge, self confidence, and the assurance that they are competent to speak out against injustice, in society and the church.

Voices of Catholic Women

Lay woman, author and journalist Angela Bonavoglia, writes on the subject of the ban on women's ordination as *central* to the patriarchal system in the Catholic Church. "It has embraced a system of *gender apartheid,* deeply hostile to women's agency, power and voice…An all-male priesthood deprives women of power by locking them out of the highest levels of leadership and decision making." This includes matters affecting women's most intimate lives, on maternity and sexuality. The irony of all this is that the vast majority of those in lay Catholic ministry are women, and that there are more women currently studying theology in seminaries than men.

As a *cradle Catholic,* she says, "It took me a long time to develop a *voice* inside that was loud enough to drown out those messages." She notes that something very important is happening today. The power of the all-male hierarchy, of the Vatican and the Bishops Conferences, is beginning to fracture. What lies in store for the Catholic Church is not certain, but the movement originating from women is not ending soon.[133] She said, "Without the incorporation of women into leadership, discipleship and all church ministries, and full participation in the liturgy—which was the vision of the (Vatican II) council—we do not experience community as women at liturgy, and we do not experience life-giving worship."

Angela spoke of the anger and rage that many Catholic women feel today, and that many of them have begun to speak out about the injustice of it all. And then she quoted a statement of Pope John Paul I, who died after only one month in office in 1978, in which he said, "We need to call God *mother* as well as *father.*" She believes that until we do that, our language and idea about God remains *exclusive, patriarchal, and militaristic.*

Sr. Theresa Kane, who recently spoke at a conference regarding women in the Catholic Church, has pointed out that "male Catholic leaders, many of them bishops and pastors, are culturally ignorant and culturally impotent regarding the presence, the potential, the human aspirations of women to be adult, mutual co-responsible collaborators. A wonderful word, *collaborate.* It means we co-labor. We are radically equal."

Benedictine Sr. Joan Chittister recently addressed American religious women in regard to the history of sisters in America. *Women and Spirit* is a traveling museum exhibit initiated by the Leadership Conference of Women Religious that reviews the story of women's religious communities in the United States. The exhibit bears witness to the role of religious life in both church and society. It is the visual history of women who made astounding choices at all the crossroads in our national history, at a time when women were allowed to make few, if any, choices at all.

These were women who opened schools for girls in a world that considered the education of women a useless waste. Many of these women nursed soldiers on both battlefields of the Civil War, North and South, in an age when sisters didn't work with men at all, much less nurse them. Some of these women worked with what was left of the Native American society that had been stripped of its dignity, robbed of its lands and denied its civil rights. Still others taught black children for centuries and then walked with them in Selma, Ala., to claim their full humanity. And overall, these women gave their lives to help Catholic children become integrated into a Protestant society as equal participants in our democratic dream.[134]

In an attempt to further the cause of religious sisters in the Catholic Church, the heads of 800 women religious congregations met in Rome May 7-11, 2010, to offer solidarity and encouragement, to share stories and generally lift each others' spirits. There is a global *sisterhood of the sisterhood* that is growing among women religious worldwide, that is crossing national, cultural and linguistic lines in a common cause to provide fresh leadership in the church. Women religious coming from Asia, New Zealand and Australia had much to share about what is taking place in their countries to help the poor and raise the consciousness of women.[135]

Other Women Leaders in the West

Most large corporations and organizations, from central government, to public sector, to professional services, have been hiring male and female employees in roughly equal numbers for some years. This has changed somewhat since the global financial crisis with the female population in these corporations and organizations slowly rising above that of the male population. However, as little as ten years ago, less than three percent of the executive directors of these companies were female, and in the largest organizations it was less than one percent.

But the world is changing and the trend is growing ever more rapidly. First, globalization has changed the markets and competition. Second, there is a social revolution going on that is changing people's expectations concerning careers and how they wish to work. A need for agility and sharper focus regarding the way people build their corporate structures is producing a steady shift away from traditional "command and control" hierarchies and a more direct linkage to markets and the consumer.

Because of these changes, evidence has been emerging that having more women at the top of organizations makes it easier to move organizations in the required directions. Since women today are the key consumers, it is necessary to listen to women in order for businesses and corporations to survive.

The Wellesley Centers for Women has reported a study based on the work of Sumru Erkut, a senior research scientist at the center, indicating that a critical mass of three or more women in the upper echelons of corporations and organizations can cause a fundamental change in the boardroom and enhance corporate governance.

"Women bring a collaborative leadership style that benefits boardroom dynamics by increasing the amount of listening, social support, and win–win problem solving." [136] They tend *not* to shy away from controversial issues, and are *more likely* than men to ask tough questions and demand direct and detailed answers. One male CEO commented, "The men feel a gender obligation to behave as though they understand everything." Women bring new issues and perspectives to the fore and broaden the content of discussions to include multiple perspectives.

Women of color add perspectives that broaden discussion even further.

This study suggests that even one woman serving on a board can make a positive contribution, and two women is an improvement. Those corporations with three or more women on their boards benefit the most. Three women normalize women directors' presence, allowing a greater opportunity to speak and contribute more freely, and men to listen with more open minds. One woman director summarized the situation, "One woman is the invisibility phase; two women is the conspiracy phase; three women is mainstream." Thus, three or more women serving on a board can create a critical mass where women are no longer seen as outsiders, but are truly able to influence the content and process of board discussions more substantially, with positive effects on the corporate governance.

Summary

This chapter has provided a number of examples that illustrate how women are becoming strong leaders in many worldwide situations. They are working to overcome serious problems ranging from civil rights issues, to renewing church policies for women religious, to initiating major changes in government and the corporate world. But women need to be prepared and educated in order to lead adequately.

In the third-world a woman's education most likely comes from life experience and the recognition of injustice in her world. Formal education helps but is not available in many instances. In first-world countries, formal education is critical. But in all cases, women leaders are those who have *found their own voice,* and have used it to develop consciousness in the ways discussed in chapter 6. In the next chapter I hope to describe the manner in which individual women prepare themselves and the steps they need to take to accomplish this.

CHAPTER EIGHT
Patriarchal Breakdown

When I ask the question, "What have thousands of years of the patriarchal system produced?" I am met with a variety of mixed outcomes. My first reply, in regard to the countries in the western world, has been the development of the alphabet, law, science, medicine and various technologies. These are positive outcomes, but there is a dark side which emerged as well. Slavery, the oppression of women, the growth of poverty, religious persecution, and the belief that *might is right* in the conquest of more peaceful societies, continued to escalate. Moreover, in more primitive tribal areas, the positive effects did *not* develop.

We discussed the archeological evidence in chapter 3 that indicates the likely beginning of the patriarchal system. Agricultural communities had already developed and were exclusively matrilineal and goddess oriented. Around 6 to 7,000 years ago warring tribes arrived from the north and east, which devastated these communities, took over control of these societies by force, and introduced male gods who gradually superseded the goddess culture. The religions which developed were male oriented, warlike, and portrayed their gods as warlords. Though goddesses still occupied the pantheon, they were eventually completely phased out and viciously suppressed. This was especially true among the Hebrews, then the Christians, and finally Muslims.

As a result, women were no longer seen as having any resemblance with the divine whatsoever. They were oppressed and a dual culture developed. Women were relegated to the home and family. Men remained on the periphery in a competitive and warlike system, and were no longer socialized in their communities to be part of the cooperative and collaborative society of the family in the manner that *women needed* to perform in order for society and culture to survive. Women became responsible for the development and maintenance of family structure and kinship, the woven fabric of culture and society.

Because a dual culture became the norm, a gender co-dependency situation developed that gradually spread to other societies. Even in India, China, and tribal Africa, where goddesses were still worshipped, this dual culture developed. Women were expected to bear and rear the children, and maintain the family system, and in return men were expected to protect the women and children, fight the tribal wars and compete for power.

Today this dual co-dependent culture is almost universal, with very few exceptions, such as the Hadza in Tanzania (Africa), and a handful of other societies found in the Artic, New Zealand, and the Amazon region. These societies live peacefully today, and the women are treated equal to men even though their daily tasks may differ. Both men and women serve their communities as partners in nearly all respects. To a great extent this partnership culture is due to the relative isolation of these groups, and is the factor responsible for maintaining their way of life.

The Betrayal of Men

What is significantly unrecognized today is the deleterious effect that the patriarchal system has had on men. In third-world countries where there is a high illiteracy rate, men tend to be members of warlike groups or tribes, controlling their communities, and abusive toward their women. In Western and more developed countries a somewhat different situation, but also disastrous, has become evident.

Susan Faludi, a Pulitzer Prize winning investigative journalist, argued in her 1991 book[137], that during the 1980s a backlash against feminism occurred due to the spread of negative stereotypes against career-minded women. She asserted that many who argue "a woman's place is in the home, looking after the kids" are hypocrites, since many men have wives who are working mothers, and many women are themselves working mothers. Much of her thinking resonates with the Jackson Katz documentary[138] cited in the previous chapter.

In her more recent book[139], Faludi turned her reporting and analysis to the problems of American men and came up with a revolutionary diagnosis. She had originally assumed that the origin of men's problems was due to what they were *doing,* rather than what was *being done to* them. By listening to men's stories in their own voices and taking them on their own terms, she uncovered a buried history that provided a genuine awakening for her.

There is a peculiar American perception, a hallmark of the patriarchal philosophy, that "men cannot be men if they are not in control *and feel it.* " Many conservative analysts have believed men are in crisis because women are challenging male dominance, and are now trying to take power and control away from them. Faludi came to understand that the problems are the product of a modern social tragedy. The untold story she describes shows how America made a set of promises to the men of the baby-boom generation, and then proceeded to break every one of them. The betrayal of the American man "has been perpetrated on many fronts, from the boardroom to the football stadium, from the military recruitment centers to the suburban living room."

A shift in the patriarchal viewpoint, which occurred in Western society, can be traced back to the Middle Ages with the rise of urban areas, the merchant class, and the crafts and guilds. These were family economies that occupied all of the family members. Family farms provided a similar living arrangement. There was a cohesiveness that worked for cooperation and collaboration among family members, and it continued for generations in the same families. When European immigrants settled in the New World and brought their economic values with them this *family economy* trend continued.

From our nation's earliest frontier days, men in the community were valued as much as the lone frontiersman—for their ability to control. But the loner was *not* the ideal. Solitude had value only insofar as it could be able to contribute to the ultimate creation of a better society. Men were especially judged by their contribution to the larger community before 1800. This was the philosophy of our nation's founders who wrote our constitution and established our form of government. Of course, this represented one of the positive aspects of the patriarchal system.

By the 19th century the Industrial Revolution began to create a *predominate* attitude regarding competition. Success in business became a compensation for loss of service to community. A philosophy of competitive individualism arose whereby American manhood gradually lost its ideal of an inner sense of self and more about acquiring possessions.[140]

The twentieth century saw a decisive breakdown in the patriarchal system worldwide, but most pronounced in Europe and America as a result of the effects of the Industrial Revolution that began a century earlier. This development increasingly distanced men from their wives, children, and homes. It became a *strategy of disconnection* which seemed to be necessary for maintaining the competitive spirit.

During the Great Depression many men lost their jobs, and their ability to be in control and to provide for their families. Because an underlying sense of economic well-being had become the social connection between men and their public life, the loss of one's job only aggravated the experience of disconnection from self and society. Many of these men actually abandoned their families. In addition, this state of affairs provided a threat to a man's sense of masculinity so that fathers no longer felt that they could be *role models* to their sons. And their sons began to sense that the lack of connection to their fathers in both personal and private ways no longer provided them *guidance* regarding how to lead a meaningful life.

The problem took a further turn for the worse after WWII due to the increasing economic abundance after the depression and war. Many of the men returning from the war no longer knew HOW to run our world and were *unable* to pass onto their sons any guidance on these matters. The *silence* that developed between them relegated the *heads* of households even more disconnected from the family *body*.[141]

In our discussion of Gilligan's research in chapter 5, we noted her reference to the *loss of voice* in both male and female children at a young age, due to the patriarchal cultural influence. She also realized that boys lost this awareness even as early as the age of four. Consequently their peer group became their mentor and provided "guidance" concerning what it meant to be a man. Usefulness to society became less important, and celebrity status increased—sexiness, renown, and winning outstripped personal worth. Even the most traditional craftsmen and community builders lived in a world where personal worth was judged as: "Am I sexy, well known and rich?" and "Did I win in my enterprise?" Yet for some men, no matter how hard they tried, there was no winning for losing in a world where they had been taught that "winning was all and losing was less than nothing."

Faludi interviewed a number of men who worked out in gyms for "body-building" purposes in an attempt to increase their physical strength and as a means of enhancing their "manliness." She noted that they were "serious gym rats, men who *lived* in the gym." Yet under the surface was still the idea that most men believed the rudimentary foundation of masculine identity is the consolation of being a steady earner. Several of these men revealed that after years of this physical activity it left them with feelings of emptiness and even further lack of personal worth.[142]

Though it seemed that many American men saw women as the enemy, they did not realize that the problem actually comes from the larger culture. Men tend to see their own diminishment due to women's strength. Faludi sees this as an *artificial femininity* manufactured by commercial interests, the same one that demeaned women for so long. It represents two sides of the same coin. Women were demeaned by *exclusion* from the realm of power-striving men, while men have been demeaned *as a result* of their powerstriving, which led them to a society saturated with competitive individualism. This robbed them of their utility and craftsmanship and ruled them by commercial values revolving around who has the most, the biggest, and the fastest—of everything. Thus both men and women were enslaved to a glamorous merchandised society.

Another problem became evident in the latter half of the 20th century when many corporations began to merge, often moving their business to other areas, producing downsizing which forced men back into the job market. This produced an anxiety about economic security, and a realization that faithfulness, dedication, and duty would no longer be rewarded in kind. Men suffered a loss of economic authority which could no longer be viewed as a masculine virtue.

Then feminism reawakened in the 1960s and 1970s after half a century of dormancy. In the 19th century women's struggle revolved around the acquisition of education and legal access, eventually culminating in the right to vote in the early 20th century. In the 1960s women came up against sex discrimination in the commercial realm. When women began to realize that they were being "sold a bill of goods" by a commercial culture, they began to revolt. Those women who struggled not to be owned by this commercialism gained a new power to stand back and see it for what it really is. This was not an easy task. [143]

The awakening that followed involved not only confrontation with the lack of career opportunities, but also with an advertising industry that had been developed to sell household products and pop psychology. The development of this "housewife market"[144] purported to give women a sense of identity, purpose, creativity, and self realization they *seemed* to lack—a mass-media and mass-merchandising cultural fraud. I recall how infuriated I felt when I read "The Stepford Wives" and later saw the movie.

Feminist critics wrote that the problem could now be named—women were being doubly used as subjects to sell products. And advertising was seen as an "insidious propaganda machine for a male supremacist society." Women were now recognizing that they were being objectified and controlled by men. But what was not recognized were the ways in which men were being controlled and objectified by the culture.[145]

At this point in her research Faludi asked the question, "Why don't men rise up in protest against their betrayal?" especially since they had experienced so many of the same injuries as women. The answer that emerged convinced her that women were framing their struggle as a battle *against* men. In their anger they used the male model of attacking the enemy—have a good fight. This has been the fundamental organizing principle in every countercultural campaign during the last half of the 20th century between religious groups, nations and the sexes.

The paradox is that this patriarchal model is the very one that men are trapped in and can't use, because the paradigm of confrontation which deteriorates into conflict, which they have defined, has proved to be worthless for men and has become exhausted. Worse yet, many women in power in the media, advertising, and the corporate world have for the most part continued to generate the same demeaning images as men. This old approach offers men nothing; a new strategy is needed. Men and women are at a historically opportune moment where they hold the key to each other's liberation and healing. Confrontation must upgrade into serious discussion, active listening, and compassion.

Raising the Consciousness of Men

Faludi sees signs that men are seeking a breakthrough. Men have begun to form groups in which they gather together, talk to each other, and seek to find workable methods. Their struggle to free themselves from their crisis is not to figure out how to be masculine, because masculinity lies in figuring out how to be human. The sense of manhood flows out of their usefulness to society. Men no longer need *to be the stereotype* or to live out the "scorecard" given by the culture. They need to find the strength and courage to face a historic opportunity to wage a battle against *no enemy,* but to act in the service of the brotherhood of all humanity.[146]

Others have witnessed this as well. Richard Rohr, a Franciscan priest, has spent twenty years working with men's groups in the U.S. and other countries.

> "(Working) with men in jails, on retreats and rites of passage, and men in spiritual direction, it has become clear and sad to me how trapped the typical Western male feels. He is trapped inside, with almost no inner universe of deep meaning to heal him or guide him. Historically, this is exactly what spirituality meant by *losing your soul.* . .The male of the species has been encouraged and rewarded for living an "outer" life of performances, which are usually framed in terms of *win or* lose."[147]

In a secular culture such as ours, there is no other meaningful storyline except one that portrays sports, contests, video games, and *proving oneself* as the way to frame the male reality. There are only winners or losers, no in-between, and little chance for growth or redemption once you are deemed, or deem yourself, a loser. Even the way the Gospel is interpreted in the Western world is primarily in terms of a reward/punishment system. There is no apparent need or concern for healing or growth or inner anything. Healing sounds "soft and needy." To Rohr, "this is a sure fire plan for having an absolutely huge shadow world and an unconscious agenda that largely calls all the shots." Just consider the context in which we find the political, Wall Street, and church scandals today.

The fact is that the church does not really encourage an inner life, whether Protestant, Catholic, or fundamentalist. The external male hierarchy interprets Scripture simplistically precisely because the American man is unwilling to feel, to suffer, to lose, and to stand in the place of others with even basic empathy. But as Rohr puts it, Jesus endured all of that, so was He a loser? How can we worship him and so idealize winning? The fact is, "we can live without success, but the soul cannot live without meaning." Rohr pleads for a way to help our men to move beyond the either-or mentality, and move into the in-between where meaning is found.

One man I interviewed, a psychotherapist who is also a former minister in the Southern Baptist Church, achieved a graduate degree at Yale Divinity School in the area of psychiatry and religion. (I will refer to him as Bob.) He worked at Yale-New Haven hospital for three years doing research for his thesis. Afterward he began a practice in upstate Connecticut and decided to go into therapy with Scott Peck, and eventually worked with Peck in his practice. Bob says, "I inherited his practice." Soon he became involved with the men's movement, influenced by such pioneers as Robert Bly and James Hillman.

Initially Bob's practice was largely composed of women and very few men. Today, at least 65% of his clients are men. He observes that most of the men he works with seem to feel that they are missing something in their lives, but do not have any idea what that "something" is. They are looking for a more peaceful life, and experience a deep sense of void or emptiness in the soul, as well as a loss of self esteem. Bob views life as a gradual unfolding process in a person. But he sees that many people, especially men, seem to stop in their unfolding, which then becomes the "missing part" that they experience.

From his experience as a psychotherapist, Bob became convinced that many, if not all, of these men can be reached by *connecting* with their inner sense of beauty, in the arts, music, and other gentle pursuits that are part of the male shadow, what Carl Jung referred to as the *anima* or feminine aspect in men. In this way they can have a new experience of their spiritual and soul elements. (We will discuss Jung's theory of the anima later in this chapter.) Bob also is quite convinced that men need to talk about their relationships with their fathers if they are to begin to unfold developmentally.

One further reference to men in psychotherapy comes from one therapist's experience helping men to achieve *connection*. The "strategy of disconnection" that so many men see as a strength, appears to be necessary for them to disavow much of the pain and sadness in their past. They simply do not wish to admit to pain, much less feel it. This is encouraged in male culture, even considered a "manly privilege." As the therapist works with his client to help him feel the pain and work through it, the client experiences shame and grief, and can often revert to alcohol and the abuse of pain medication. This therapist believes that the center of treatment is the trust that must develop between the client and his therapist.[148] The connection between them is what promotes healing, but even though it is necessary, it is often not sufficient.

The Ravages of War

Nothing has betrayed men more than war. According to Edward Tick[149], a psychotherapist who has worked with the survivors of war for over twenty years, "war is a living archetype inherent to the psyche." I believe it is the archetype of the patriarchal system which dates back to the conquest of agricultural communities more than 6,000 years ago. But there were warring tribes prior to this, perhaps as long as 10,000 years back in time. We have no archeological data about these tribal origins, only that they historically appeared in the Middle East suddenly and drastically changed those societies. The war archetype took over.

Because humanity basically still operates according to the ancient belief of an "eye for an eye", even though we are taught today that this is morally wrong, the tendency is to seek punishment and revenge on those who have hurt us. In war chaos overcomes compassion, violence replaces cooperation, instinct replaces rationality, and gut dominates mind.

The Experience of Loss of Identity

The damage experienced by humanity because of war, especially to males, takes three forms. First is the enormous death toll to the troops as well as to those peoples considered as the enemy; second, the vast number of those with physical wounds who will no longer be able to live normal productive lives; and third, those troops who return with wounded *souls* because of what is now known as post-traumatic stress disorder (PTSD). There is further evidence that more and more female troops are experiencing PTSD as well. Even though women are not permitted to participate in the horrors of frontline battle, they nevertheless often experience the results of it as medics or members of rescue teams.[150]

PTSD is best understood as an identity disorder and soul wound affecting the personality at the deepest levels. The soul is disfigured often for life. Such a loss is an extreme psycho-spiritual condition beyond what is commonly called dissociation. And it is more than psychic numbing. "It is a removal of the center of experience from the living body without completely snapping the connection. In the presence of overwhelming life-threatening violence, the soul or true self flees."[151]

Following is a list of some of the ways that *soul* has been conceptualized:

- Soul is the drive to create and preserve life.
- Soul is the awareness of oneself as a discrete entity in time and space.
- Soul is our intellectual power that thinks, reasons, and understands.
- Soul is what gives us our ethical sensibilities, the spirit behind the moral code of the Ten Commandments.
- Soul is our will, our individual volition.
- Soul is our aesthetic sensibility that hungers, perceives, and appreciates beauty.
- Soul is the part of us that loves and seeks intimacy.
- Soul is the seat of imagination that functions to make and interpret images.
- Soul is the great cry of *I AM* that awakens in the person.
- Soul contains the shadow—those aspects judged unacceptable by society, religion, or self.[152]

The Journey to the Underworld

When speaking of the damages brought on by war, Tick notes that if something hurts so much that it feels like it tears a hole in the heart, a person experiences himself as meaningless, senseless, and no longer knowing who he is. In working with PTSD patients he frequently heard the pain expressed as "I've lost my soul." The journey back to self is full of confusion, anguish, ordeals, loneliness, grief, mistakes, and harmful pride.

Dr. Tick has spent decades learning to negotiate the *inner world* of war survivors and to map it, so that veterans could find their ways through the damage toward healing. Those who work with these patients in the healing process, as well as their loved ones, need to have an effective guide for facilitating their veterans' "homecoming."[153] Many of these veterans remain jobless and homeless for the rest of their lives, frequently as alcoholics or drug addicts.[154]

Because PTSD is an identity disorder and soul wound, the need is to move from the war/warrior archetype and to develop the *spiritual warrior,* which enables the ability to confront the soul that has been lost in the "Underworld." The journey back requires the courage to go within, to deal with one's shadow, in order to find the true self or soul with the help of another archetype that lies hidden in the shadow—the *inner prophet.* It is the spiritual warrior that enables the descent into the depths of the self. It must be done imaginatively in a supportive community so as to *feel* what was forbidden to feel on the battlefield. Healing only occurs by reliving memories and their accompanying feelings so as to *relieve* them and let them go in forgiveness. This is a type of spiritual surgery. Instead of living stuck in the horror of hell, one *consciously returns* to it for the purpose of understanding it. Then only can there be a *return* from the "Underworld."

Saying "yes" to this secondary imaginary descent is often the most difficult step, yet it is an act that restores the essential affirmation of the soul: I AM! Each horror and death of a *brother* must be brought to consciousness, grieved, and laid to rest. Gradually this process enables the survivor to feel that he has a right to live a full life. A healing journey of this type can allow PTSD to evaporate because the truth has been revealed and the heart is freed from the bondage of the past.[155]

The process of engaging the *spiritual warrior* can be viewed as an initiation leading to a fully developed personality. The survivor learns to carry his war skills and vision in mature ways, inwardly, in respect to the full realization of his manhood. In this way he will be set right again, to protect life, his own and others, rather than to destroy it. He will learn to serve his nation in peace so as to dissuade others from suffering the scourges of war. Fearlessness will develop to help keep sanity, generosity, and order alive in his culture. He will learn to discipline the violence within, and to serve spiritual and moral principles that are *higher* than himself.[156]

A number of investigative journalists have uncovered other aspects of war damage to veterans as well as to those who are considered the "enemy." A recent study[157] revealed that in California more than 1,000 veterans under 35 have died after returning home from Iraq and Afghanistan between 2005 and 2008. This represents three-times more than California service members who were killed in conflict overseas, according to a recently published Bay Citizen report. Some of these deaths are attributed to suicide, while others result from high risk behavior such as motorcycle and motor vehicle accidents and accidental poisoning. Veterans are two and one-half times more likely to commit suicide than Californians of the same age who have not served in the military.

Another study of the effects of war on Afghanistan natives[158] describes an interview with a young man who had been a good student and had enjoyed his studies. Now, at age 22, he says, "I can't seem to think now. War does this to your mind." He tells how his family fled their village, his father was killed, and other Afghan ethnic groups discriminated against them. He has struggled with depression that was so serious that he felt ready to give up on life. A local youth group, the "Afghan Youth Peace Volunteers," and some friends and community members have helped him come to terms with his pain to assure him that he can find a meaningful future. Stories like this are repeated again and again.

How Myth Has Maintained the Warrior Archetype.

Myths are the universal stories about our deepest human experience, repeated in every generation since antiquity. All religions are rooted in myth so that they seem to have been sent by Divine Revelation. Myth is not fantasy or "make-believe." Rather, it is truth conveyed in metaphor and archetypically imbedded in the human psyche or soul. It is innate to all of us. Myth underlies all rituals and rites of passage, and each culture manifests specific versions of these universal patterns.[159]

In Greece, Heraclites believed that opposition, including competition and strife, are built into the very nature of the cosmos. Only some survive the conflict because nothing lasts. Everything eventually disappears through death or transformation. This idea is similar to what was presented in Chapter 1 regarding *chaos theory* and even Darwin's concept of survival of the fittest. Both clashing and striving can be used for good or ill, for or against self and other, to inspire us either to excel or destroy. There are two poles of our relationship to war: greed, frenzy, and bloodlust vs. restraint, strategy, and grief.[160]

All early mythologies proposed that war originated because of Divine will. The god whose people triumphed was the true deity with the most righteous followers, while those who were defeated were unholy and their deity was false. The concept of Holy War evolved out of this early religious history. This was well established in Jewish culture, later in the early Christian era, and followed hundreds of years later in Islamic tradition. Holy War became an expression of God's will and that God chooses rulers to express his will. Eventually this idea developed into the concept of Just War; the power to declare war should be in the hands of those who hold supreme authority descended from God. Unjust wars would be fueled by the intent to do harm, a desire for vengeance, revolt or lust for power.

Tick recognizes that we cannot or will not surrender our belief that supports war as long as we believe it is God's will; the myth and the archetypes are too strong. The question is, "are we intelligent or diplomatic enough to make war obsolete?" He claims that as a people we do not hate the state of war, in fact, we crave the state of being it offers. It enhances our nationalistic causes. The false notion that war protects our nation and its interests allows us to accept the sacrifice of husbands, sons, and daughters to confront "terrorists" and defend the world against grave danger. Thus, we fail to correct our mythologizing, and we elevate our lost loved ones to heroic status, and ignore the suffering to our antagonists as well as ourselves. It seems that we are stuck in the archetype and myth.[161]

The Gender Co-dependency Dilemma

The reason humanity has been bogged down in the war myth for so many thousands of years is due to the vastly different ways males and females have been socialized, and the gender co-dependency that has resulted. Both men and women must participate in the overthrow of the patriarchal system.. But their journeys are very different.

At this point I wish to briefly review the material presented in Chapter 5 regarding the work of Carol Gilligan and Robert Kegan. While women are *finding their voices* (Kegan stage 3 → 4) men are still enmeshed in a competitive environment that betrays them and increasingly threatens all of us. We need to find a way to help men move into cooperative and compassionate relationships with others, and most importantly with themselves. I mentioned that the shift from K-3 to K-4 for women, (and those men who have decisively reached K-3), could not be predicted for a person with any accuracy in regard to age. In fact, it appears that many never accomplish it.

This K-3 to K-4 transition requires a spiritual or contemplative evolution that begins with a desire within a person to dialogue inwardly with herself or himself. A deeper focus on nature and the environment, and how an individual fits into this schema, can be a beginning. Life-long self-perceptions programmed by others in childhood can be understood in new and healthier ways. Psychotherapy can certainly help in the assessment of feelings, especially regarding marital and family relational issues.

But unless a person begins to reprocess this information inwardly, in a spiritual way, regarding his or her own sense of self, their efforts will not generate new Kegan self structures.[162] What is worse, most men have remained stuck in K-2, the competitive stage that does not yet respond to stage K-3 cooperation, collaboration, and compassion in interpersonal relationships. Spiritual evolution requires an attention to Self-understanding that is oriented *beyond* the small and false self that has been heretofore known. It is much like the contemplative discipline of the 12-steps used in Alcoholics Anonymous and Alanon groups. Let us look at one possible method of understanding this dilemma.

C. G. Jung's Understanding of the Masculine and Feminine

Carl Jung, the Swiss medical doctor and psychiatrist, who founded the school of analytical psychology, developed his own contemplative methods for Self-discovery and understanding. He recognized that the human psyche was comprised of many characteristics, which he called *complexes*. Most of these complexes are hidden in what he called the unconscious. In addition, much of this unrecognized element of the psyche was not acceptable to a person. He referred to this hidden material as the *shadow.*

Further insights into the mystery of the male/female cultural duality also come from his work. Jung[163] came to believe that there is a strong feminine quality to the human *soul,* which exists as an inherited psychic complex residing in the shadow unconscious. He viewed this as *especially* true of men. He called this feminine quality *anima,* and saw it as a source of genuine wisdom.

> "No man is so entirely masculine that he has nothing feminine in him. The fact is, rather, that very masculine men have—carefully guarded and hidden—a very soft emotional life, often incorrectly described as 'feminine.' A man counts it a virtue to repress his feminine traits as much as possible, just as a woman, at least until recently, considered it unbecoming to be 'mannish.' The repression of feminine traits and inclinations naturally causes these contra-sexual demands to accumulate in the unconscious."[164]

Jung would agree with Gilligan's concept regarding the *loss of voice* in males, even as early as age four, that stems from a repression of the male identification with the mother. Girls, in contrast, having maintained their identification with mother well into adolescence, have lost their identification with father. So the loss of identification with mother in males, as well as the loss of identification with father in females, results in this hidden contra-sexual aspect of the psyche in both genders.

Jung saw that the feminine aspect in men (anima) was more troublesome and less well defined than the corresponding aspect (animus) in women. It seemed to him that the anima was very difficult for a man to access, and more likely to be avoided altogether, and tended to be projected outward on to women.

On the other hand, the *animus* in a woman eventually *imposed* itself on the female consciousness, not as an image, but in words. Jung's wife Emma observed that woman's experience seemed to indicate that this *voice* would comment on every situation in her life, frequently imparting applicable rules of behavior. Writing toward the end of her life (d. 1955), she observed that this voice expresses itself chiefly in two ways:

> "First, we hear from it a critical, usually negative comment on every movement, an exact examination of all motives and intentions, which naturally always causes feelings of inferiority, and tends to nip in the bud all initiative and every wish for self-expression. From time to time this same voice may also dispense exaggerated praise, and the results of these extremes of judgment is that one oscillates to and fro between the consciousness of complete futility and a blown-up sense of one's value and importance. The animus' second way of speaking is confined more or less exclusively to issuing commands or prohibitions, and to pronouncing generally accepted viewpoints." [165]

Emma Jung's analysis foresaw what the Belenky[166] research team uncovered in regard to *women's ways of knowing* (Chapter 6). They described and categorized exactly what Emma had observed in regard to the unconscious activity of the animus. The process of evolutionary growth that this team described is precisely the story of how a woman emerges from the conscious and unconscious programming of the patriarchal culture.

Because feminine energy tends to move inward, (women especially are aware of this in the more introverted experience of pregnancy), and masculine energy seeks to move outward, we see in men a tendency to expend their energy in their jobs and careers. At the same time they ignore their feminine energy, which is inclined to draw them inward to introspection and contemplation. There is an experiential gap in their psychic experience in that the feminine aspect (anima) wants to pull them inward, while at the same time their natural tendency is to move outward and ignore the inward pull.

From a Jungian standpoint, it is now clear to me why men up to this point in time have found it so difficult to consciously contact and address their feminine side. We witness this outward movement of male energy especially in science and technology, and various business endeavors today. For women, on the other hand, the tendency to draw inward, pondering their experience for the sake of others, inclines them to experience what is moving *within* the psyche. Their masculine energy (animus), always seeking to move outward, is more likely to meet their feminine aspect and begin an inner partnership. Thus there is naturally much less of a gap between the masculine and feminine energies in women. But women must be encouraged to express this, because until recently their wisdom has not been given voice and valued. Because only the male experience has been validated, men do not accept or even recognize their own "inner partnership".

It is women, hopefully, who will become able to teach their men about the need to achieve an inner balance. Those men who have accomplished this feat function beautifully in their relationships and find easy access to their inner wisdom. Conversely, women who have worked through their negative animus experiences become truly strong and capable of egalitarian relationships. All traces of wanting to dominate disappear and they are able to empathize with the male struggle. And the gender co-dependency dilemma gradually subsides in favor of partnership between men and women.

Summary

In this chapter we have examined the male side of the patriarchal "coin." Men have been demeaned, betrayed, and seriously damaged by this system, at the same time that they have demeaned and oppressed women. This has been a cultural problem for thousands of years and has only started to break down in the 20th century. The patriarchal system is in rapid decline today and there is a concomitant resistance to change, because our entire view of "how things are supposed to be" is being drastically upset. But progress is on its way nonetheless. We shall examine the manner in which we need to change in the next chapter.

PART THREE
Spiritual Evolution

CHAPTER NINE
the Return to Spirituality

When we consider the enormous span of time since the Big Bang, roughly 14 billion years, and recognize that we knew almost nothing about the evolutionary process until the last century, it boggles the mind. We can only understand evolution by looking *backward* at the evidence presented by science and technology, yet we must live the future evolution of humanity in a *forward* manner. And we will never know what life might have been like on our planet during most of the four billion years of the earth's existence, much less what it might have been like to live in the universe *before* the earth was formed. We can only imagine and guess about this.

In addition, we are at odds with *ourselves* at the present time because we are enmeshed in a chaotic period that is attempting to push us into the next phase of human evolution. And we are meeting and causing ourselves much resistance because we are unable to imagine where we are going. This new evolutionary phase is already here, but we are unable to grasp its meaning as yet, and we feel threatened by it. Chaos has overtaken everything.

Examples of systemic problems include: our economic and financial situations, joblessness and poverty; wars and threats of war, nuclear arms proliferation; our educational system; our marriages and families, depression and an increase in the rate of suicide; our religious systems; pollution of the environment because of technological advances, the need for new and more efficient recycling methods, and global warming leading to ever greater possibility of famine and disease. And all of these boil down to one thing, the breakdown of the patriarchal system.

The philosophy behind this system, encompassing male dominance, competition, and a disregard for the intrinsic connection of all things in our global experience, has produced a massive splintering in regard to ways to solve the multiplicity of our problems. Because all these difficulties are symptoms of a much larger problem, it is important that we grasp what is needed to advance evolutionarily as human beings in order to gain some insight into all these areas.

Some people believe we need to retrieve old "tried and true" methods from the past. The problem with this approach is that it has been tried but is no longer "true." It will not produce new ways of thinking, and certainly, no new ways of dealing with the issues that confront us. The innate evolutionary *wisdom,* which we need to employ in order to solve or resolve these chaotic areas, seems out of our reach, and we have lost a sense of meaning in regard to it. We do not understand how to access this wisdom, yet we already possess it, hidden deeply within our spirits.

I have presented evidence in chapter 7 regarding ways in which women are breaking out of the gender co-dependency to which they've adhered for thousands of years. This is happening everywhere, on a worldwide scale. Women would not be coming forward in this manner if it were not for a renewed awareness and impetus coming from Divine Wisdom/Sophia, the feminine aspect of God. Yet the patriarchal philosophy strongly resists this divine aspect in most men and many women.

On the other hand, the evidence presented in chapter 8 points to a growing awareness in men and women that the patriarchal system has failed to answer our questions and heal our pain. Men are feeling thwarted, and many males are resorting to greed and violence, often against women, in an attempt to once again feel "powerful."

There are many groups related to the environment, conservation, and saving endangered species that are making some advances in regard to our disconnection from nature. The purpose of one group[167] "is to return to the nation's children what they don't even know they've lost: their connection to the natural world." Again, Divine Wisdom, "the Hidden Heart of the Cosmos"[168] is at work in raising our consciousness regarding these issues.

Biblical Teachings about Divine Wisdom

The Sacred Scriptures from both the Hebrew and Christian traditions provide us with wisdom insights. For example, from the Hebrew Scriptures we find:

> "Wisdom is bright and does not grow dim.
> By those who love her she is readily seen,
> and found by those who look for her.
> Quick to anticipate those who desire her,
> she makes herself known to them.
> Watch for her early and you will have no trouble;
> *you will find her sitting at your gates.*
> Even to think about her is understanding full grown;
> be on the alert for her and anxiety will quickly leave you.
> She herself walks about looking for those who are worthy
> of her and graciously shows herself to them as they go,
> in every thought of theirs coming to meet them."
>
> (Wis. 6:12–17)

This passage speaks of the hidden character of Sophia/Wisdom, as well as her ever-present nature, "sitting at my gate". It is interesting that the Hebrew Scriptures refer to Wisdom as feminine, a divine aspect forever existing with God from the very beginning. Rabbi Shapiro[169] even refers to it as the Divine Feminine. I believe that this is the essential, innate programming that guides the evolutionary process.

The Christian Scriptures (New Testament) are full of references to the Kingdom of God. Just a few of the gospel passages teach:

- "The kingdom is close at hand." (Mt 10:8)
- "The kingdom of heaven is like a merchant looking for fine pearls; when he finds one of great value he goes and sells everything he owns and buys it." (Mt 13:46)
- "The kingdom of God is among you." (Lu 17:21) This is often translated as *the kingdom is within you.*

- "It is easier for a camel to pass through the eye of a needle than for a rich man to enter the kingdom of heaven." (Lu 19:24)

These scriptures tell us that the kingdom of God is near; it can be found within and among us; it is like a *pearl of great price;* and is difficult to enter if we are consumed by worldly riches. They echo the passage above from the Book of Wisdom. My own belief is that the kingdom is the *inner place* where Wisdom is found. It is at the center of our being where the evolutionary teachings are to be discovered. The difficulty lies in how to access it. [170]

A Return to the Spiritual

In order to access the kingdom where Divine Wisdom is to be discovered we must learn how to reclaim our spirituality, a psychic function present in the human *experience* for at least 70,000 years. Spirituality is a *relational* function with self, other human beings, nature and God. It is about a deeply felt experience of *connection* with all that is—the entire universe. Spirituality is an inherent energy which belongs to the evolutionary unfolding of creation itself, and it embodies the evolutionary Wisdom that guides this energy.

Diarmuid O'Murchu[171], a social psychologist and Catholic priest, points out that "spirituality concerns an ancient and primal search for meaning that is as old as humanity itself…it belongs—as an inherent energy—to the evolutionary unfolding of creation itself." Today spirituality tends to be perceived as a subsystem or offshoot of formal religion. In fact it has always been more central to human experience than formal religion which can be traced back *only* 4,500 years.

To O'Murchu, the religious, moral, and spiritual breakdown confronting us today has to do with a breakdown of religion and not spirituality. We fail to grasp the real issues or name them in a creative way. Our religious traditions have become irrelevant for many; at the very least they do not provide the kind of creative insights we need to resolve our dilemmas. Rather, he sees that we need to take our evolutionary unfolding seriously so that we can transcend what has previously existed in order to grow into an enlightened future. O'Murchu is not focused on abandoning anything, but instead on expanding our vision so as to evolve toward what is beckoning us forward. In the process our religious traditions and practices will be revitalized at a deeper level. They, too, will have evolved. [172]

Reclaiming spirituality involves the practice of contemplation—of pondering one's experience, of all that is, *in depth*. There are several forms that contemplation may take: the contemplation of nature; the study of sacred scriptures; gaining self-understanding through personal reflection or therapy; finding ways to work through relational difficulties with spouses, family members, and friends; and developing a conversational and experiential relationship with the Divine Presence within—at the center of the True Self. All of these varieties require the breakdown of *disconnection* so evident in the patriarchal system.

C. S Lewis[173] once wrote that God whispers to us in our joys and pleasures; God speaks in our experience of conscience; and God shouts at us in our pain. He saw that pain offers the last resort to humanity for hearing God's voice. Pain presents an opportunity for a person to experience a *dark night of the soul* [174], in which a person can *find light* in the darkness by searching for new meaning. Often, when other forms of contemplation have failed or been avoided, darkness will usher in the beginning of another form of contemplation. I am convinced that we are experiencing a planetary "dark night" that is forcing us to awaken to the dangers of our time.

Brian Swimme points out that we need to *confront* the power of the advertiser that promulgates a world-view, a mini-cosmology, that is based upon dissatisfaction and craving. Advertisement has become our culture's primary vehicle for providing our children with their personal cosmologies, instead of the spiritual wisdom that is emerging from science in regard to evolution. He further quotes a cliché, "an ad's job is to make them unhappy with what they have." Thus, consumerism has become the dominant world-faith in every continent on our planet today, and humanity has come to believe that men and women *exist to work at jobs, to earn money, to get stuff.*" "It is just too horrible to think that we live in a culture that has replaced authentic spiritual development with the advertisement's crass materialism."[175]

Therefore, all forms of contemplation represent the *beginning* of a new evolutionary phase in human consciousness—a return to spirituality. To this end the stages and phases of the human life cycle are being examined today by many people for genuine, evolutionary possibilities. Eastern philosophies, which have long focused on the uses of disciplined experiences, like meditation and contemplation, as exercises of consciousness for self-development, have been divested of many religious elements that lead to and maintain conservative beliefs. They have become secular tools for the advancement of self-knowledge in everyday life. This is a move in the right direction toward evolutionary transformation.

At some point in mental development meditation and contemplation become *possible*—exactly when has not been determined. Dream analysis and focusing on the meaning of what one feels can also be useful. But it is not a question of "one size fits all." What works for one may not work for others. It is necessary for each unique individual to learn which practice best produces new information that leads to transformational change. For the most part, this requires the exploration and "re-membering" or *reconnection* with unconscious material.

Models of Spirituality

There are a number of models of spirituality that have appeared in the last century which look at the characteristics of the human psyche, yet include traditional teachings from classical religious wisdom of centuries past. Among those who emphasize methods which help the discovery and development of contemplation, as a form of attaining self-understanding and *reconnection,* are the transpersonal theorists. The term *transpersonal* refers to the ways in which meditation and contemplation open the human mind, beyond mere ego-stages, to an ever greater perception of levels of reality, the spiritual realm. These theorists, like Kegan, are rooted in a developmental stage perspective, but they go beyond the merely psychological stages into the domain of mystics and holy men and women throughout the ages. The following models share many similarities, their differences arising primarily from variations in the focus on the overall issue. In some cases different terms are used to express the same reality.

Wilber's Perspective

Among the most important of these theorists is Ken Wilber, who writes primarily from the spiritual teachings of Buddhist philosophy and practice. Wilber quotes St. Bonaventure, a Doctor of the Catholic Church and a mystic, who taught that men and women have at least three methods of attaining knowledge. Bonaventure called this the "three eyes of the soul." He described these as the *eye of flesh,* the senses by which we perceive the external world of space, time, and objects; the *eye of reason,* by which we attain the knowledge of philosophy, logic, and other areas of the mind; and the *eye of contemplation,* by which we rise to a knowledge of transcendent realities. [176] This "third eye" *requires* the use of what is referred to as *intuition* or extrasensory perception.

Wilber's way of interpreting the "eyes of the soul" is to address the first and second *eyes* in the classic manner of developmental psychology, and the higher stages of consciousness, *the third eye,* as taught in the Buddhist tradition. Like Kegan, his developmental stages are viewed as building upon one another. In other words, each new developmental level will subsume previous ones, so that none of them are ever lost but may be reverted to under certain circumstances. If we compare Wilber's stages with those of Kegan (see Appendix E) we can view his higher stages[177] as surpassing Kegan stage 4. Wilber's final three transpersonal stages, I believe, are encompassed in the K-4 to K-5 transition, and probably beyond, which Kegan does not describe. These "higher" stages are contemplative ones which result from the enlargement of *third eye* perception into the *depths* of spirituality.

Analytical Psychology

Carl Jung's work took the concept of the three eyes into account when he recognized the *four functions* of consciousness. He saw that both the senses (eye of flesh) and the intuition (eye of contemplation) were *perceptual* functions. On the other hand, the eye of reason, by which we judge our experience, is composed of two functions, *feeling and intellect.* Jung also recognized that there were sixteen types of personality depending on which of the four functions were preferred, or predominant, and whether the person was introverted or extraverted.[178] In addition, he saw that a person would develop psychologically over time if and when the four functions became increasingly integrated.

In a very early essay[179] Jung used a metaphor about the rising of the sun in the morning, to reaching its peak around noon, and then the descent in the afternoon toward night, as a description of the stages of human life. Essentially, as a person develops, it becomes necessary for *consciousness* to gradually take over "that which *nature* has always done for her children—namely, to give a certain, unquestionable and unequivocal decision." Problems arise which demand that we determine the solutions through growing consciousness and our own efforts.

> "When we must deal with problems, we instinctively refuse to try the way that leads through darkness and obscurity. We wish to hear only of unequivocal results, and completely forget that these results can only be brought about when we have ventured into and emerged again from the darkness. But to penetrate the darkness we must summon all the powers of enlightenment that consciousness can offer…we must even indulge in speculations."[180]

For Jung there are no *real* problems in the childish stage of consciousness because consciousness has not yet been completely born. This newly emerging stage only begins to appear at puberty. Thus, there are truly no problems without consciousness. It is only in the state of inner tension, which occurs when one impulse opposes itself to another, that the person *feels* at odds with himself and recognizes that there is a problem.

In Jung's discussion of the development of more mature consciousness, he describes three phases: first, the recognition that one is experiencing a chaotic mental state; second, the development of the ego-complex in which one recognizes his lone responsibility to deal with the situation; and third, one's awareness of a divided state, a dualistic phase. These phases continue to exert themselves throughout the youthful years following puberty, up until the *noon-time of life.*[181]

Roughly around the age of forty the "sun begins its descent" in the human life. Jung notes that "the descent means the reversal of all the ideals and values that were cherished in the morning (of life). The sun (ego) falls into contradiction with itself." By the age of fifty one's plans are usually falling apart. What has broken down is the masculine style of life (patriarchal values) which had been maintained by one's preoccupation with past experience and values. Jung's advice is that "we cannot live the afternoon of life according to the program of life's morning—for what was great in the morning will be little at evening, and what in the morning was true will at evening have become a lie."[182] It is the true Self that is beginning to manifest.

Jung believed that the true Self lay hidden in the personal unconscious which was fed by what he called the collective unconscious. Moreover, the Self was continuously attempting to make itself conscious through the circumstances a person encountered in life. He also believed that God dwelled in the collective unconscious, which was so closely united with the personal unconscious that once a person became aware of the Self, he or she could not differentiate between God and the Self.

As early as 1933, well before World War II, Jung saw that "the spiritual problem of modern man is one of those questions which belong so intimately to the present in which we are living…and has to do with something so universal that it exceeds the grasp of any human being." He saw that the only man who is truly modern is the one who is *fully* conscious of the present. "Only the man (person) who has outgrown the stages of consciousness belonging to the past and has *amply* fulfilled the duties appointed for him by his world, can achieve a full consciousness of the present."[183]

Jung recognized two important facts about humanity: first, that "much of the evil in the world is due to the fact that man in general is hopelessly unconscious"; and second, "that with increasing insight we can combat this evil at its source *in ourselves.*" The discussion in chapter 8 concerning PTSD, more and more recognized in returning military personnel today, echoes what Jung saw after WWI when he wrote this essay—*modern man in search of a soul.*

In regard to religion he noted that as long as humans live from a *herd-mentality* one has no "things of the spirit" of his own. "But as soon as he has outgrown whatever local form of religion he was born to—as soon as this religion can no longer embrace his life in all its fullness—then the psyche becomes something in its own right which cannot be dealt with by the measures of the Church alone.[184] In this way Jung gave preference to *conscience* over religious form and rules.

The Dynamic Ground

It is clear that Jung's contribution to transpersonal theory is immense, as a chief pioneer and a towering figure in the field. This is the opinion of Michael Washburn,[185] a professor of philosophy, who developed a Jungian, Christian, and psychoanalytic approach to the transpersonal dimension. He presents a developmental system that contains strong spiritual elements. Much like Wilber, Washburn defines transpersonal theory as the study of human nature and development with the assumption that human beings possess potentialities that *surpass* the limits of the normally developed ego. It presupposes that the ego, as ordinarily constituted, can be transcended and that a higher, *transegoic* plane or stage of life is possible. He views transpersonal theory as a multidisciplinary inquiry aimed at a *holistic* understanding of human nature.

But unlike Wilber, who speaks of the transformative process as a linear path, Washburn sees the necessity of taking a U-turn somewhere down the line in life's journey. Washburn postulates that the ego exists in essential relation to a superior *Dynamic Ground* and that the *highest possible* psychic organization is one in which the ego, itself fully developed and self-responsible, is a faithful instrument of this Ground.[186] The chief objective of transpersonal theory is to integrate *spiritual experience* within a larger understanding of the human psyche. It is a project that attempts a true synthesis of spiritual *and* psychological approaches to the psyche, a synthesis that involves a thorough rethinking of each of these approaches in terms of the other.

Washburn's approach is a dynamic-dialectical paradigm that revolves around three aspects. First, a bipolar constitution of the psyche consists of a nonegoic or dynamic pole which is characterized by energy, instinct, spontaneous feelings, and sensuality. This pole corresponds to the concept of the collective unconscious in Jung's theory. In contrast to the nonegoic pole Washburn describes the egoic pole as being reflexive, abstract, can use self-control, and cultivates the personality. This pole has a bimodal structure that is both active and receptive in its functionality. Washburn notes that the egoic pole (ego) is in its active mode when engaged and in command of operational functions. In its receptive mode it is disengaged and open to nonegoic influences. Thus, in its active mode the ego is individuated and asserts itself, whereas in its receptive mode it is dependent upon the nonegoic pole.[187]

The second aspect of his paradigm is a dialectical interplay between the two psychic poles. In Washburn's approach the nonegoic pole alone is active in the *neonatal* period; the egoic pole exists at first only as a potential and is dormant and undifferentiated. However, in a very short time the egoic pole begins to be activated and to differentiate itself, becoming involved in the developmental process and remaining involved thereafter. Even though the nonegoic pole remains dominant for some time during the developmental process, the ego gradually frees itself from this domination by alienating the nonegoic pole and banishing its potentials from consciousness. Thus the movement toward the full egoic stage, while it is a developmental advance, is paid for by the retardation of nonegoic life. Washburn refers to this process as the *original repression* of the Dynamic Ground.[188]

The third aspect in Washburn's model of the psyche maintains that selfhood unfolds according to the bipolar and dialectical perspectives. The nonegoic pole is believed to be the ultimate and higher self, the egoic pole being the subordinate and lesser self. As the ego develops, the psyche becomes divided and separated from the wisdom and evolutionary energy of the Ground.[189] At this point the character of the ego/Ground interaction is drastically altered, and the power of the Ground is for the most part restricted to the status of the libido, the energy of the instincts. However, the Ground continues to affect the ego primarily through transferences and projections onto other persons or situations.

During the mature years of the second half of life the Ground may on occasion break loose and manifest itself as religious or mystical experience. In this way, the early repression of the Ground which began with the beginning of ego development, can gradually give way to a "regression (to the Ground) in the service of transcendence." The ego begins to confront the Ground within the intimacy of the soul, and a battle ensues to determine which of these will become the sovereign power of the soul.

The ego experiences this encounter as with an alien force and attempts to banish it from consciousness. A Dark Night of the Soul may begin with greater or lesser intensity. And so, similar to Jung's position regarding the descent of the ego in the second half of life, the egoic pole will eventually experience a need to *consciously* return to the Ground in order to investigate these matters, thus gradually uniting with the primordial Self in order to profit from its Wisdom. [190]

For Washburn, the integration of the ego with the Ground is best accomplished by the approach of meditation/contemplation because it "pursues the straightest and truest course" to the unconscious.

> "When consciousness is occupied with worldly affairs, it is blind to most of the stimuli that arise from or are latent within…However, when meditation disengages attention from external concerns, it at the same time interiorizes awareness, rendering consciousness observant of inner signals."

Because meditation introverts the attention it makes the meditator aware of the stream of consciousness that is ordinarily experienced as the *background noise* of life, which consists primarily of the internal dialogue of the mental ego. [191]

Nevertheless, meditation as a technique or specific exercise really comes to an end once the Dynamic Ground is opened to consciousness. Meditation is like "drilling for oil" which is a long and difficult process.

But with perseverance the meditator will "strike oil" when it recognizes the power of the Dynamic Ground. Once this has occurred Washburn feels it is no longer necessary to practice meditation exercises, but rather to yield to the transformative process that is unfolding within.[192]

The Underground River of God

One further model of spirituality I wish to discuss is presented by Fr. David Hassel, SJ.[194] He describes four levels of conscious awareness. First, the *Sensuous-Superficial,* which is the sensual experience of minor irritations and pleasures, such as hunger pangs and annoying sounds, or the appreciation of a favorite meal or the smell of roses.

The second level, the *Physical-Vital,* represents the awareness of more intense pain and joy, such as a headache or the effect of insomnia, as well as the enjoyment of a Bach symphony or sexual ecstasy, or the experience of relationships with others. These second level experiences "com-penetrate" and influence the first level of sensuous awareness.

Hassel's third level, the *Psychological-Psychic,* is defined by experiences that elicit strong emotion, such as deep sorrows and pure joys. These can so permeate one's consciousness as to render it unaware of first- or second-level happenings. Anger, depression, deep feelings of insecurity, or loss of self-esteem can very readily clog one's awareness of duties and other agendas. But eventually the first two levels will be integrated into the third level and given fuller meaning. This is the level where awareness of the past and need for healing will surface.

Hassel refers to the fourth and deepest level as the *Underground River of God.* This level corresponds to Washburn's concept of the Dynamic Ground and Jung's idea of the Self. Hassel says it quietly nourishes the upper three levels, "sustains them in their storms and bliss" and acts as the sustaining power underneath their rapid fluctuation. "This fourth level is never explicitly conscious in itself—as are the top three levels—but only by way of contrast."[195] It is implicitly experiential. In fact, this level enables the person to gain a quiet and peaceful perspective on the other three levels. It is as though one is aware of *witnessing* life from a deeper level that sheds light on all experience.

This fourth level of peace and security brings a sense of God's love. The discovery of this level often comes during some kind of *dark night* experience, which opens up a new revelation of self, and others, and God. New meaning for life comes into being. This is the level of Divine Wisdom and evolutionary transformation. It "contains the center of one's universe" (the Self), "the hope of one's total future, and the source of one's strength to love when not loved back."

The experience of the fourth level is one of flooding up into the top three levels and may give added physical energy, bring about creative activity, and lend stability to one's thinking, imagining, feeling, and decisions. It is also the level where "discernment of spirits" is experienced, that is, an assurance of God's will for the individual. It can frequently result in a sense of joy and lightness of heart. On the other hand, a sense of uneasiness can cause disturbance and be a sign that one's decisions must be reevaluated. The important realization is that a strong sense of God's love is present to prepare the way.

The fourth level is the experience of contemplation which then permeates the top three levels and enters into all the activities issuing from them. Prayer at this level gives new alertness of God's presence in others, a renewed hope in people's future fidelity, and a deeper confidence in God's providence. A spiritual director may prove helpful in discerning the effects of this level of prayer. There is no doubt that this level is a mystical and transformative one.[196]

Through my own research and work with clients I have observed that there is a definite relationship between psychological development and spiritual growth. However, the relationship does not appear to be completely symmetrical. I realized that psychological development does not *necessarily* lead to spiritual growth. On the other hand, spiritual growth is very likely to encourage psychological development. When I compared Hassel's four levels of awareness with Kegan's developmental scheme, I found that there was a very recognizable equivalency.

- The K-1→K-2 stages correspond to Hassel's *Sensuous-Superficial* level which represents a preoccupation with the external world and attaining some kind of control over it, that is common to young children. Keep in mind that these stages do not disappear but are subsumed by the next higher stage as are Hassel's awareness levels.

- K-2→K-3 is similar to Hassel's *Physical-Vital* level because the focus is no longer merely on one's own needs, but rather focuses on the emotional response to the environment, which includes interpersonal relationships and the *need* to adjust to them for greater balance and harmony.

- K-3→K-4 corresponds to Hassel's *Psychological-Psychic* level where the focus is on past performance, its triumphs and failures, the need for personal healing, and finding new and deeper meaning for one's life and self.

The movement beyond K-4 toward the K-5 stage enables a person to know him or herself more objectively as well as to recognize other persons as "other selves." Like Hassel's *Underground River of God,* one must adapt toward experiencing one's center. It involves an experience of "breaking free" from family, cultural norms, and prejudice, and toward accepting others for who they are. Greater harmony and peace are commonly experienced and achieved in this way.

As long as a person simply knows the "self system" subjectively at K4 the greater Self is not known. Only the beginnings of contemplation and the inflow of the "underground river" can initiate further psychological development toward K-5 and the discoveries that go beyond the individual ego.

Summary

Today the need is for a *spiritual evolution,* one that goes beyond ego and individualism to a recognition that we belong to the universe and *must* be responsible to it and to each other. We must plumb the depths of our innate, hidden, evolutionary Wisdom. We must become *transpersonal.* The models of spirituality discussed in this chapter present a multifaceted picture of what we need to do to evolve as the human race. The ability to do this is already imbedded in the human psyche just waiting to be discovered and initiated.

We must listen to the deepest center of ourselves, to the *feminine wisdom* of the soul inherent and hidden in our common humanity, both males and females alike, as opposed to the patriarchal philosophy dominant for so many thousands of years. Women will need to learn how to overcome their anger at their current situations, and to help their men and boys to become interpersonally relational and cooperative members of family and society. We shall look at the effects of this spiritual evolution in the next chapter.

CHAPTER TEN
Spiritual Healing and Evolutionary Transformation

*I*n the previous chapter I described several evolutionary models of the transformative journey taught from a variety of disciplines—Buddhist and Christian perspectives, a philosopher's view, and the psychoanalytic approach of Carl Jung. In this chapter I wish to describe the *actual experience* of evolutionary transformation, as it impacts persons, and the results of it in their lives.

Spiritual evolution is pushing *and* pulling the human race forward worldwide. As more people develop the ability to contemplate the inner Divine Wisdom, the stronger the pull will be. They will be transformed by the evolutionary energy, and become potential models and mentors to the rest of humanity. It is already happening, but we do not yet have a critical mass.

Contemplation is the means whereby we become aware of the Sophia/Wisdom energy that is divinely implanted in the human psyche. But this energy must be discovered by an act of *conscious* desire to find new meaning for our life experience. There is *monastic* contemplation practiced by monks and contemplative orders of women. And there is the kind of contemplation that the ordinary person may experience when attempting to reevaluate his or her lifestyle. Either way, the result is contact with the Divine Wisdom energy and the likelihood that a person will encounter God, however one names it. This is known as the revelation of the Divine within the Self.

What is most important in this matter is: contemplation must evolve into action on the part of the one who contemplates. In the Sacred Scriptures Jesus says:

> "I am the vine, you are the branches. Whoever remains in me, with me in him, bears fruit in plenty; for cut off from me you can do nothing. Anyone who does not remain in me is like a branch that has been thrown away—he withers...It is to the glory of my Father that *you should bear much fruit.*" (John 15: 5-6, 8)

If we translate this passage in terms of the models discussed in chapter 9, remaining *in Christ* refers to the surrender to one's True Self, the Divine image. This is how Jesus was able to live and teach pure Wisdom. The True Self is what Jung saw as the dwelling place of God and the vine coincides with Washburn's concept of the Dynamic Ground. Remaining in Christ constitutes a freely chosen, consistent contact with the True Self and the Dynamic Ground.

Bearing fruit signifies that there is an internal effect, proceeding from the knowledge and wisdom received in contemplation, which *demands* to be used. Wisdom not used is merely knowledge. Wisdom only bears fruit when it manifests in action. That is its *evolutionary* purpose and power.

Awakening the Heart

The contemplative experience required to change one's life seems to occur in a fashion described by both Jung and Washburn in the previous chapter. A person must turn inward and begin to rethink his values in light of ongoing experience. Psychiatrist Gerald May, says, "Both neurological and contemplative evidence point out an essential truth about *awakening:* because desire awakens us, our wakefulness is always *for* something; it has a direction."

Contemplatives go further than the neurologists; they describe a quality of consciousness existing in the *absence* of stimulation and creative impulses, during moments of inner quiet, for the love of *being* itself. It requires a growing and intensive period of *questioning* that eventually becomes more or less permanent. It is consistent questioning that is needed to bring about contemplation which leads to human evolution today.

Dr. May claims that contemplatives recognize a deep level at which every heart is always saying yes to love. This is true regardless of how dulled and preoccupied our conscious minds are, or how unloving are our actions. It is not so much conversion of heart as a conversion of consciousness or a *metanoia* in which we awaken in order to *turn and intend* our attention toward what our hearts have desired all along—love.[196] He believes we are meant to participate in love without really understanding it, by giving ourselves into love's mystery.

Constance Fitzgerald,[197] a Carmelite theologian, writes:

> …"the Dark Night brings dryness, boredom, and absence of satisfaction, and removes the very support systems that have structured our lives, given them meaning and value, and provided a source of affirmation and final assurance… The time will come when our philosophy of life, our theology, and our carefully constructed meanings fall apart before our eyes. All we have accumulated intellectually that has given us God, faith, and security loses its significance. Nothing makes any sense."

Often there is emotional pain and severe doubts about one's values. This has been described by St. John of the Cross[198], a Carmelite of the 16th century. He referred to this experience as a *Dark Night of the Soul,* which begins a period of questioning and reaching out for *Something* beyond ourselves that might answer our questions.

Abandonment and a betrayal of trust are the hallmarks of this dark experience, and often the most cherished persons in our life seem to be cut off or taken away. This loss of love from a loved one becomes the cause of the worst agony that occurs during the darkness. We feel isolated and sense that no one else can understand our predicament. And we do not understand our predicament either. Furthermore, there is a profound fear of this unknown evolutionary process.

What is occurring is the beginning of *faith,* no longer in ourselves or our beliefs, but in *Something* or *Someone* we do not yet know. It seems to work at cross purposes with our ability to make logical sense out of life. This is what Wilber referred to as the opening of the eye of contemplation or the *third eye.* It is an intuitive experience that does not come from any information outside the sensory self or from worldly wisdom.

Hopelessness and emptiness eventually give way to the realization that one can no longer struggle against the darkness. A self-surrender occurs bringing *hope* that there is a way out of the misery, and the *hope* that the way out comes from within the depths of the person.

Dr. May takes his cue from Brother Lawrence, a 17th century monk, who taught the *practice of presence.*[199] This monk's teaching has become a classical treatise on the four steps in practicing presence, or contemplation: remembering, heart prayer, relationship, and contemplative presence or prayer. These practices lead to Wisdom. The Dark Night was the manner in which my own contemplative experience began. I wept and suffered confusion and abandonment severely for nearly nine months. It was another year and a half afterward before I felt I was finally out of the darkness. And my worldview had changed. Later when I had reached a greater clarity about my situation, the teachings of Brother Lawrence became relevant and very helpful. While I am not particularly recommending this type of *monastic* contemplation, to a large extent, regardless of how the process begins, the *effects* are similar. The heart is awakened and transformation begins.

Our planet is experiencing a Dark Night today. If we are to survive we must evolve. And if we are to evolve we *must descend* into our inner depths to develop a *new approach* to life—encountering and utilizing our inner Wisdom. At this point in our evolution there is a gradual emergence of Sophia/Wisdom, the feminine aspect of God. (Sophia is the Greek word for Wisdom). Fitzgerald recognizes the correlation between the intense interest in the Dark Night, the awareness of Sophia, and the emergence of feminism, just as there was a correlation in the past between the muting of contemplation, the suppression of Sophia/Wisdom, and the marginalization of women. She believes that Sophia represents the God-image that resonates with the current state of the collective psyche. This *hidden* Wisdom is being revealed.

Remembering

Brother Lawrence's method for finding Wisdom begins with remembering, which he called the *little interior glance.* This involves uncovering the unconscious material Washburn describes as "forgotten" in the development of the ego—the U-turn that will reunite the ego with the Dynamic Ground. May asserts that because there are many situations in and around us that *force* us into forgetting, our decision needs to be one of consciously stretching toward God and yielding into a hopeful receptivity that *God will remind us of God*—or put another way—allowing Wisdom to remind us of our need for Wisdom. Dr. May reminds us that God is always trustworthy, but resolutions and willpower are not.

Prayer time, worship services, or gathering with friends who have a similar interest are all approaches that help us to remember God's presence. May also suggests deliberately looking for the presence of the Divine in other people by paying close attention to their words and actions. And he advises looking at ways our daily activities at work, travel, and recreation, as well as our experience of nature, may remind us of God rather than become occasions for forgetting.[200]

Heart Prayer

Recitation of mantras, sacred syllables or phrases repeated silently or aloud, was evident in Hindu practice thousands of years ago and became an integral part of Buddhist spirituality, while the Islamic Sufis, in the eighth century, began the practice of constantly reciting the names of God. In Christianity, the *Jesus Prayer* came into practice in the fourth century. These practices help to maintain the decision to remember God. During times of worship or remembering, a particular word or image will "install" a practice that can be returned to at will and reinforces remembering as a habit. For some people observing their breathing can serve as an aid to their practice. With sufficient repetition the prayer or mantra becomes a natural part of oneself, truly a prayer of the heart.

Relationship

May is convinced that whether we are distracted or not, whether we know it or not, whether we even *want* it or not, a communication between the soul and God keeps going on beneath the surface of our self awareness. It is always there. There is nothing we have to do to make it happen, nor can we escape from it. It is a relationship with the source of love, with the *Ground of our Being.* The great majority of religious people have some notion of this relationship, but most do not recognize it as natural and normal for all human beings. [201] Brother Lawrence referred to it as conversation with God.

Contemplative Presence

Dr. May agrees with Brother Lawrence that it is in contemplative presence that we appreciate *reality*—the actual world—most directly and accurately. Brother Lawrence called it a *pure gaze* that finds God everywhere. May says, "In consecrated contemplative presence, there is no question of whether one is attending to God or to something else." He sees that everything is present in God and God in it. We are alive in it, part of it, yet simultaneously every bit of who we are—we are absolutely involved.[202]

It is important that we *not* make a distinction between contemplation and action. Many people automatically associate contemplation with quiet stillness and action with concerted movement. The contemplative option does not make the separation from action to begin with. Though traditional forms of contemplative prayer are usually taught in an atmosphere of relaxation, it is also necessary to assume that it involves wakefulness. It can come as a gift, a moment that arises into *conscious awareness.* If one can be authentically responsive to grace in this moment, no practice is necessary; you are simply *living in love.*

When you are letting yourself be who you are before God, then the "you" that is experiencing includes everything in you that is true and natural. This includes knowledge, experience, the ability to judge and to choose, common sense, responsiveness, and the ability to act. You will neither suppress your own natural activities, nor simply follow every impulse that comes. Because of one's consecration, nothing happens outside of or apart from the concern for love.[203]

Engaging Evolutionary Wisdom

An important question in our discussion is: Why don't more people engage the inner Wisdom which has been evolutionarily programmed into the human psyche from the beginning of time? Robert Kegan[204] believes that because we have *other agenda,* most of which are deeply rooted in our perceptions, assumptions and former ways of thinking, we find it difficult, if not impossible, to find new meaning to apply to our issues in the present moment. He claims that "modern man is in over his head"[205] when it comes to finding new ways to solve or resolve his problems. This kind of difficulty is experienced daily on a worldwide level in *every aspect* of human existence these days.

The difficulty is that as long as we attempt to deal with our issues from culturally maintained principles, we will not be able to think beyond them. We will continue to return to the old ways. Yet, there is a saying that if we "change our way of thinking we will change our lives", because what is changed is our worldview—a new way of *seeing* our lives. The truth is: we cannot find Wisdom unless we know we need it. This requires a change of *agenda,* personally and collectively.

I have repeatedly described how the dominant manifestation of the patriarchal system, for the majority of males, is one of individualism, competition, and a preoccupation with wealth and "success." Patriarchy is also inclined toward war and violence and is likely to be *empire* oriented. The following stories are centered on the *contemplative experience* of two men and two women who have changed their life agendas in regard to the military, war and the betterment of others. Their transformation stories are genuine.

Andrew Bacevich

Andrew[206] describes the difficulties inherent in his lived agenda:

> "Worldly ambition inhibits true learning. Ask me. I know.
> A young man in a hurry is nearly uneducable. He knows
> what he wants and where he is headed; when it comes
> to looking back or entertaining heretical thoughts, he
> has neither the time nor the inclination. All that counts
> is that he is going somewhere. Only as ambition wanes
> does education become possible...My own education did
> not commence until I had reached middle age. I can fix
> its start date with precision; for me, education began in
> Berlin, on a winter's evening, at the Brandenburg Gate,
> not long after the Berlin Wall had fallen."

He goes on to describe how, as an officer in the U.S. Army, he began to *contemplate* the German agenda in WWII. He saw how the futility of war had reduced East Germany to a third-world country. Bacevich further describes his experience: "Uninvited and unexpected, subversive forces had begun to infiltrate my consciousness. Bit by bit my worldview started to crumble." He was not so naïve to believe that the American war record had been without flaws, but he assured himself that any errors or misjudgments had been committed in good faith. For him the United States had simply done what needed doing. And the Cold War had played a crucial role in sustaining that worldview.

Thus nearly 45 years after WWII, the end of the Cold War, and the Berlin Wall had fallen, his life changed dramatically when his military career ended after 23 years in the army. Many questions came to mind and he felt forced to *contemplate* them deeply. He found contradictions in the decision of the US, an ostensibly "peace-loving nation", to commit itself to a doctrine of "preventive war" by going into Iraq twice during the 1990s. Bacevich saw that there was not the "foggiest notion" of what victory would look like in an ill-defined and open-ended "global war on terror". Finally he realized that the worldview to which he had adhered as a young adult Army officer, and then carried into middle age, had dissolved completely. Today Bacevich notes:

> "Fixing Iraq or Afghanistan ends up taking precedence over fixing Cleveland and Detroit. Purporting to support the troops in their crusade to free the world obviates any obligation to assess the implications of how Americans themselves choose to exercise freedom…When Americans demonstrate a willingness to engage seriously with others, combined with the courage to engage seriously with themselves, then real educations just might begin."

Basevich now believes that "more often than not what passes for conventional wisdom is simply wrong. Adopting fashionable attitudes to demonstrate one's trustworthiness…is akin to engaging in prostitution." He is now dedicating himself to exposing these ideas especially in regard to the assumptions, habits, and precepts that have defined the political ideology and the tradition of the United States. To this end he has written his book, *Washington Rules,* in order to verify this situation to the American public. He is also writing online as an independent journalist to inform the general population on these matters.

Floyd Meshad

Forty years ago when Floyd "Shad" Meshad[207] was serving in Vietnam, as a psychiatric social worker, he witnessed the horrible effects of battle on our soldiers as well as on the Vietnamese. He found that the image of God he had built up during his years in Catholic school did not fit. How could God stand by and allow this? Working with casualties in a M.A.S.H.unit, he recalls "swimming through blood, doing tracheotomies, and holding screaming soldiers as they were dying… All a psych officer could offer was a Band-Aid…some peace of mind, moments of peace." Wounded when his helicopter was shot down, Shad felt abandoned by God.

After one year in Vietnam, Meshad came home to a sense of anger, alienation, and a feeling of emptiness. Back with his family, his mind was still in Vietnam, disturbed and confused by his dreams, thinking he was still there. He was in the emotional state described by psychotherapist Edward Tick[208] in chapter 8. At one point Shad felt a need to find a new environment, and he drove to Los Angeles.

Today he says, "God guided me." Within two days of arriving in Los Angeles, he was introduced to the head of psychiatry at the Brentwood Veterans Administration Hospital, who wanted Meshad to evaluate the facility and talk to him about the vets he was seeing.

While working at Brentwood, Meshad was running his own operation: street ministry with homeless vets, holding rap sessions, and working with PTSD patients. Two years into this experience he realized he had found a new life, and he began to find God again. He saw that he had a mission to these veterans, not a religious one, but spiritual nonetheless. He realized that Vietnam represented man's inhumanity to man.

Eventually Shad founded the National Veterans Foundation, which connects vets and their families with vital services and utilizes a toll-free number to that end. For over 24 years he has provided services ranging from crisis counseling and benefits assistance to transportation and job training. He calls this foundation "an instrument of my consciousness, a product of this intense desire I have to give back. It's not a church, but we minister. The spirit gets lighter. And that helps people make good choices—the choice to go another day and another."

It is very clear to Shad that there are no winners in war. He is thankful everyday that he has been given this work to do. Instead of having a wife he says, "I married my work." Today he is one of the nation's top experts on combat stress, trauma therapy, and the readjustment issues that veterans and their families face. To have experienced the horrors of Vietnam and survived, and to have found God again, makes him one of the fortunate ones, he feels.

Laura Turkington

I first met Laura's husband, Brian, while I was studying for my MS degree in marital and family therapy. He became my supervisor during my internship. I spent two years working with him in his psychothera-peutic practice. In addition to being an excellent therapist, Brian was also an ordained minister in the Congregational Church of Christ. He was divorced with no children from his previous marriage. He and I became friends as well as colleagues.

It wasn't long before my husband and I became friends with Laura, too. The interesting fact about their marriage was that Laura was Jewish and had two sons, from a previous marriage, teenagers who had celebrated their bar mitzvahs. It was obvious to us that Brian and Laura's religious dif-ferences seemed to blend easily. My husband and I were very fond of them and shared many memorable occasions. The four of us remained close.

After awhile Brian closed his private practice and took another posi-tion as program director at an alcoholic rehabilitation center in another town. I began to work with clients in my home while continuing to study for another MS degree in behavioral research.

Some ten years later, Brian and Laura decided to move to Florida. Brian worked again as a therapist, mentor, and counselor, offering classes and worship services to those in one of the residential facilities where he practiced. Laura held employment in business. Her children had also moved to Florida and the couple was involved with them and the grandchildren. We visited them a few years later—our one and only trip to Florida. Still we kept in touch via mail, e-mail, and telephone.

Brian died in 2010, after a seven month struggle with brain cancer. Laura resigned her job as soon as Brian was diagnosed and devoted her-self to him. During his last days at hospice, difficult as they were, Laura became aware that life as she had known it was changing irrevocably. She would no longer be responsible for anyone but herself, and she realized that when your life changes you must change your way of life. During the hospice experience, both Laura and Brian became aware of a strong spiritual message—hospice would be where she would spend a portion of her new life. "God had given me a plan for recovery from the loss and pain of the previous seven months." She is in counseling with a bereavement counselor who is helping her with the grieving process, and in training to become a volunteer for hospice.

I wanted to tell Laura's story because it illustrates how she changed her agenda because of the difficulty and pain she endured. It is typical of the change that comes from *contemplating* one's situation. Her life has become more spiritual, but not in a well-defined religious sense. Laura simply knows that God is leading her in this new way. Her goal is to give back the love and support that she received to others who are experiencing the kind of suffering she endured.

Maureen Dowd

In a 2010 op-ed piece, columnist Maureen Dowd of the New York Times, described her experience while in Saudi Arabia.[209] She had been having tea with a group of educated and sophisticated young professional women. She wrote:

> "I asked why they were not more upset about living in a country where women's rights were strangled, an inbred and autocratic state more like an archaic men's club than a modern nation. They told me, somewhat defensively, that the kingdom was moving at its own pace, glacial as that seemed to outsiders. How could such spirited women, smart and successful on every level, acquiesce in their own subordination? I was puzzling over that one when it hit me. As a Catholic woman, I was doing the same thing. I, too, belonged to an inbred and wealthy men's club cloistered behind walls and disdaining modernity."

Maureen was speaking about the patriarchal system that still operates in the Catholic church. She saw that she, too, remained part of an autocratic society that repressed women and ignored their progress in a secular world. Even though the problem exists in all the churches to some extent, in the Catholic Church it is blatant. Not only does she refer to the sexual abuse scandal involving priests with boys and girls, Maureen speaks of how the Vatican is generally avoiding a discussion on many topics regarding women. Yet only women's experience of God can alter or renew our God images and perhaps our doctrine of God.

Recently the question of the ordination of women has brought a Vatican condemnation which states, that even for a woman to *seek* ordination, is a *grave crime* against the church. And it brings an automatic excommunication on such a woman. In addition, women in religious orders have been investigated by the Vatican in regard to their ministries in which they have diligently worked to implement the mandates of Vatican Council II over the years.

Today feminists struggle with the Judeo-Christian image of a male God and a male Church. Feminists see a patriarchal system that visualizes God, and consequently the Church, in almost exclusively patriarchal terms, as basically destructive.

It is difficult to assess the degree to which contemplation of their life experience has transformed these four persons. But at the very least they have taken an important step in that direction. All of them were brought into deeper relationships and into a more profound understanding of the human condition, by contemplating the suffering of others. They came up against the violence of war, the suffering of the sick, and the injustices of patriarchy and saw the effects. In the long run, their worldviews were drastically changed and they chose to teach their views to other suffering souls in their own unique ways. This is the kind of agenda shift that produces evolutionary change and is becoming more and more necessary for all of us.

The Collective Evolutionary Shift

Though the above stories illustrate how individual people have experienced a change in their worldview, Riane Eisler's[210] seminal work describes what an evolutionary worldview shift will mean *collectively* for our culture and worldwide. It is a seminal book concerning what needs to be accomplished in order to transform the whole of humanity. She proposes an evolutionary leap that affects our relationships with one another in our families, our government, our corporations, businesses, banking, educational and healthcare systems. In her book she reflects on how her own worldview shifted and her agenda changed.

Riane was born in Austria. As a young child she and her parents left Vienna, fleeing from the Nazis, and arrived in the slums of Havana, Cuba. Sometime later the family moved to the U.S. where she grew up. She reports feeling as though she were on a quest most of her life. The burning question seemed to be, "Why, when we humans have such a great capacity for caring, consciousness, and creativity, has our world seen so much cruelty, insensitivity, and destructiveness?"

She speaks of her discontent in this way:

> "I used to think there wasn't anything I could do to make
> ours a better world. I didn't even think there was much I
> could do to change things that made me unhappy in my
> day-to-day life. But I found out that I was wrong on both
> counts."

Growing up in the German cultural mode that professed the role of women to be "Kinder, Kuche, und Kirche" (Children, Kitchen, and Church), Riane began to develop a new consciousness of how the *gender double standard* had constricted her life and that of other women. (My own experience of living in the ethnic German culture resonates with hers.) She describes the change that occurred:

> "Once I freed myself from the dominator trance [patri-
> archal philosophy], from the stories I had been taught
> [what] is the natural order and my natural place in it as a
> woman, my consciousness, my energy, and my life took off
> in directions I never thought possible. From feeling hel-
> pless and overwhelmed, I moved into an action mode—
> including social and political action."[211]

Riane looked for answers to her persistent question in many areas. She pursued psychology, history, anthropology, education, economics, and politics. In the experience of rearing her children, and later in observing her grandchildren, her worldview shifted, and she settled on an economic viewpoint. This new perspective grew out of her thirty years of research applying evolutionary systems science and *chaos and complexity theory* to social systems. She notes that this allowed her to develop and apply an updated view of *evolution* to our global problems.[212]

Eisler began training in legal matters and founded the Los Angeles Women's Legal Program, the first U.S. program on women and the law. She offered lectures on the discrimination against women, legal at that time, as well as providing free legal services to poor women. Using her legal training, she wrote a Friend of the Court brief to the United States Supreme Court, making the then-radical argument that women should be considered persons under the Equal Protection clause of the Fourteenth Amendment to the Constitution, and that laws discriminating on the basis of sex should be struck down. Her efforts, coupled with those of other women and men, succeeded.

However, Riane gradually began to understand that changing laws was not sufficient, and that we must go deeper to fundamental cultural and structural change. She conducted a cross-cultural and historical analysis, focusing on the relationships between women and men and parents and children. The configurations that emerged were twofold: a new economic system of partnership caring for the common good, and the patriarchal domination system. She recognized that these two configurations affect our habits of thinking, feeling, and acting. Our families, religions, economics, and politics are affected, as well as the stories we live and die by. Furthermore, numerous research studies have shown that the configurations of these two systems affect "nothing less than the development of our brains."[213]

Riane has recognized that the current economic system, based on the patriarchal philosophy, is unsustainable. To prevent economic and ecological collapse we must restructure the global economy, implement a comprehensive poverty eradication strategy, and restore damaged ecological systems. Nevertheless, even if these essential changes are effectively implemented—which seems doubtful under present norms and rules—new crises will inevitably erupt. We are living through a period of *evolutionary chaos* that has occurred again and again over the ages in many areas on our planet, in order to facilitate the move to the next human developmental level.

We urgently need changes in the economic rules guiding the market, because the middle class and the poor often end up paying the cost of uncaring business practices. Riane sees that one way to do this is to tax stock market speculation. She puts it this way:

> "Under present economic rules, people are supposed to serve the needs of the market as workers and consumers. This is backward. Economic rules should ensure that the market serves our needs as human beings living on an increasingly threatened planet."[214]

Both structural changes and values must contribute to changing economic rules. Government and business leaders must see to it that economic indicators include the essential work of caring and care-giving performed in the household and the unpaid community economy. The costs of environmentally and socially destructive products and activities must also be a factor. Government and business leaders must go further toward encouraging and supporting caring and care-giving activities.

Riane notes that what lies behind the devaluation of caring and care-giving is the gender double standard that ranks men and the stereotypically masculine over women and what is perceived as feminine. For her the ultimate goal of these economic changes is the development of the human capabilities of each person. She is urgent about accelerating the shift to partnership cultures and structures worldwide so that caring is given higher value.

Much of what Eisler has acknowledged comes from digging into the research of others from many fields. Viewing other data from her economic standpoint, she realized that a partnership system is considerably less expensive for both government and business in the long run. From a purely financial cost-benefit perspective, a shift to a partnership and caring culture is one of the best investments a nation can make. After all is said and done, the real wealth of a nation lies in the quality of its human and natural capital, an investment in human beings. Currently the United States has no coherent policy for investing in human capital.[215]

What are the dynamics of transformation to a caring partnership system? A caring revolution will necessitate a cumulative effect, rippling from many directions, into an economic perspective. In a world where economic systems are what they should be and can be, human needs and aspirations are sure to be met. Riane comments:

> "As the general quality of human capital rises, more capable, skilled, and caring workers contribute to a more productive economy...This makes more funding available for government and business policies that support caring and care-giving. And this in turn enhances the quality of life for all."

As the market economy gradually changes, businesses will reward more caring behaviors. They will recognize that employees who feel cared for are more productive and that customers who feel more cared for are more loyal. Government policies that support caring will recognize a sound and essential investment. Problems that seemed intractable will begin to wane, and poverty and hunger will be more effectively addressed. And finally, along with the higher values given the life-sustaining activities of the household will come a higher valuing of the life-sustaining activities of nature.[216] This transformational shift in society will bring with it an evolutionary shift for all humanity. We must all become part of it.

Intergenerational Healing

My own habit of digging into the research of those who have gathered data in other disciplines has not only confirmed my own data, but has also given me new insight into the *meaning* of some of my data. In the late summer of 2000 I was invited to give a presentation at a symposium in Toledo, Ohio on the topic of intergenerational healing. [217] The attendees at this symposium consisted of persons, some of them clergy, who served as liaisons to their bishops for the Catholic Charismatic renewal.

Intergenerational healing necessarily takes into account a number of factors. I considered the experiential conditions, the developmental states of readiness, and the psychological and spiritual effects that produce this healing. Intergenerational healing was not a specified topic in my research, but it was easy to find relevant material in my data to delineate the topic. The material I presented was grounded in my research with women as I experienced it in three separate contexts: 1) my own life story, 2) my clients, and 3) the women whom I interviewed in depth in for my doctoral dissertation. While each of these contexts is distinct, similar patterns emerged in all three. Life-span histories (including early family life, education, and religious training), personal crises, psycho-spiritual growth, and ongoing lifestyle conversion all play a part in a person's journey. In addition, cultural factors place women in a unique position to be *midwives* for development in others.

Kegan's developmental stages were pivotal in determining the readiness for relational and cultural change in the women I encountered. (See Appendix B.) At stage K-3 the women were still ensnared with gender co-dependency. Not until development had solidly moved toward K-4 could a woman gain even an *inkling* regarding *contemplation* of her life experience and personality characteristics in such a way that could make possible a shift in her worldview.

However, as long as a person maintains equilibrium after reaching K-4 consciousness, that person will not continue to evolve. The requirement of adaptation to experiencing one's center where the "underground river" flows, will not occur. The initiation into contemplation truly takes place only with development beyond the K-4 equilibrium toward K-5, the truly spiritual realm. This is the evolutionary movement in which the person soon discovers that there is a *breaking-free* from family and cultural norms, even bondage, and that she or he is becoming an instrument of change in their environment. One of the benefits of this personal developmental shift is the increasing ability to accept others as they are, free of prejudice and contempt.

Intergenerational Healing Challenges

The Christian message is not about adjustment, competition, or worldly success (K-2 consciousness) but rather about maintaining the common good (K-3 at least), which Eisler demonstrates and advocates in her book. But herein lies the problem. With men predominantly at the K-2 developmental level, and women carrying the burden of caring and care-giving while maintaining a co-dependant relationship with men, the evolutionary change cannot take place, or is very difficult at best. We must deal with a number of issues and challenges.

Both men and women must recognize the culturally constructed developmental differences into which most of them have been socialized and are currently locked. Both men and women need "space" in order to gain some understanding of how they have perpetuated this dissonance personally and culturally. Men need to develop the interpersonal, mutually oriented communication skills (K-2→K-3), and women must learn how to work through their "co-dependency" issues and come to know themselves as persons with individual life paths.

A new approach to spirituality and religious practice will be needed. Men will have to gradually become *interpersonally* committed to God. Women will need to become serious about relying on the Holy Spirit, and their inner Wisdom, to seek and ask for daily Divine guidance in their lives. For women, "submission of wives to husbands" will be replaced by submission to God in her situation with her husband.

The Forgiveness process

Forgiveness must become a way of life. Forgiveness is a means of *deconstructing* the effects of one's past experience and creating new meaning in the present. Indeed, without forgiveness new meaning *cannot* be found. It is a necessary choice for personal, relational, and intergenerational healing. The process of forgiveness described by the women in my research is best described as a series of steps.

1. During the initial experience of anger and hurt brought on by a perceived injury, there is usually an attempt to ease the pain in one or more ways:
   a) trying to distract oneself by becoming very busy with numerous tasks;
   b) trying to forget what has happened; c) trying to discover *why* the situation happened.

2. When the troublesome emotions reoccurred, a woman usually began to pray in the following ways: a) for herself to gain the courage to *actually* forgive the person who hurt her; b) for the person who caused the injury, so that he/she could receive the forgiveness and perhaps become repentant. Usually these praying episodes are repeated multiple times before any sense of progress has been made.

3. The praying step may eventually produce a certain determination to let go of the resentment toward the one who has caused the injury. This involves an inner dialogue and struggle that may last weeks, months, or even longer, depending on the severity of the injury. The beginnings of *contemplation* may enter one's activity at this point.

4. The person may begin to ask, "Did I do something that hurt the other person?" This may begin the process of self-forgiveness, as well as an attempt to accept the other just as he or she is, in spite of what has happened.

5. Attempts to return to the relationship are frequently made in the hope of improving or restoring it. This may not be possible in some cases, yet making the attempt is considered extremely important when the injuring party is a family member or has previously been a close friend.

6. The above five-step process may have to begin again, especially if the negative feelings keep occurring. This forgiveness process, though difficult and prolonged, necessarily involves new meaning-making, as well as the capacity to understand both self and other more completely. It offers the possibility of a new worldview and

an opportunity to change one's agenda. In studying the women in my sample, I recognized that truly forgiving another brings the forgiver peace of mind, a new sense of well-being. Permanently releasing the negative emotions is an integral part of the developmental transition from K-3→K-4.

I concluded that without forgiveness new meaning *cannot* be found. If a person is not able to dispel the illusions about the self necessary for true self-understanding, the true Self will not be encountered. Forgiveness is one important way to contact the hidden Wisdom, the underground River of God, the Ground of Being that accelerates personal evolution. Experiencing this psychological realm enables awareness of the process that is gradually changing the person including:

1. That there is a self-identity that is still growing;
2. That the person is becoming desirous of "letting go of control" in life;
3. That truth lies within the self;
4. That it is a struggle to become authentically oneself;
5. That one is becoming a seeker on a soul journey;
6. That the person is becoming a compassionate companion to others;
7. That there is recognition of becoming a healer in one's family.

The ability to attain this kind of personal awareness of the workings of the psychological realm leads to a new religious practice, as described by Gerald May and Constance Fitzgerald earlier in this chapter. This is evolutionary spirituality that gradually transforms the person from the image of God, mentioned in the creation story in the book of Genesis, into a *likeness to God*. From this "higher" self-understanding the person becomes an instrument or channel of generational healing, within the family and society, and to intergenerational healing, stretching back into past generations and into the future.

Constance Fitzgerald[218] notes that if we deal with personal impasse during the Dark Night only in the manner our society teaches us, we will deal with societal impasse in the same way. We will not be able to find any escape from the world we have built (the patriarchal system), where the poor and oppressed cry out, where the earth and environment cry out, and where the specter of nuclear weapons and environmental waste already haunt future generations.

Fitzgerald already saw in the mid-1990s that our world was experiencing a *societal impasse* or planetary Dark Night. She said:

> "We stand helpless, confused, and guilty before the insurmountable problems of our world. We dare not let the full import of the impasse even come to complete consciousness...Is it possible these insoluble crises are signs of passage or transition in our national development and in the evolution of humanity? Is it possible we are going through a fundamental evolutionary change and transcendence, and crisis is the birthplace and learning process for a new consciousness and harmony?...Our impasses do not yield to the logical solutions of the past, to the knowledge and skills acquired in our educational institutions... the economic solutions of past decades do not fit the present economic crisis...Not only God and the loved one(s) fail us, our institutions fail us."[219]

Fitzgerald's view was that if we refuse to read the signs of Dark Night in our society and avoid appropriating the impasse, we will only use our cold reason, devoid of imagination, and head toward violence, hardness in the face of misery, and a sense of inevitability regarding war and death. Furthermore, it seemed to her that we dare not believe that a creative re-visioning of our world is possible.[220]

What a prophetic grasp she had! Today we see it before our very eyes, and it is frightening. We need to form a society of caring and care-giving that Eisler has described based on her research. Ideology based on past experience will surely fail us. We need to pay attention to what history has to teach us and to what our inner Wisdom wants to give us as a solution.

Summary

This chapter has emphasized the necessity of developing a contemplative attitude toward our personal experience as well as toward the crises in the world today. We have finally become aware of the chaos that is pushing us to an entirely new strategy for world peace and intergenerational healing. It is our evolutionary heritage rising from our deepest Wisdom and bringing with it a cosmic leap for humanity.

Afterword

Chapter 10 was about half written when it became necessary for me to have open heart surgery to repair the mitral valve. The surgery was done in the beginning of May and was very successful. However, there were many setbacks that caused a major delay in healing. Within two days of the surgery I was literally "thrown" into constant atrial fibrillation. In spite of two cardio-versions (shocks) and heavy amounts of medication, the fibrillation could not be controlled.

Eleven days after the surgery I went to a rehabilitation facility. The staff there did not understand my situation, so that two weeks later I was back in the hospital. I received two more shocks and it was determined that I should have a pacemaker/defibrillator implanted. I developed a urinary infection as well as phlebitis in my left arm from an IV port, and was sent back to rehab to wait for the pacemaker surgery with a prescription for a strong antibiotic to address the urinary and phlebitis infections.

The pacemaker procedure was performed in another hospital, and after two days I was sent back to rehab with more of the same antibiotic to insure that the implant healing would be safeguarded from infection. I did not return home until two months after the first surgery. I was in a very weak and depleted condition, much of which was caused by loss of appetite. I lost nearly 30 pounds in body weight and appeared very gaunt. A neurological condition in my right leg developed, called "drop foot" which made it impossible to lift that foot. This condition required more than six weeks of physical therapy, several times a week. Because of the foot problem I had to learn to walk all over again, delaying the resumption of driving the car as well. I also had weekly visits from nurses, occupational therapists, and a home health aide who gave me sit-down showers. Thank God for the Visiting Nurse Association!

To complicate the situation, my husband had a medical emergency involving his right knee two weeks after my heart valve surgery. He couldn't stand or walk and was sent to the same rehab facility where I was lodged. Apparently he had ruptured a ligament so that he spent two weeks in rehab before he moved in with one of our sons and his wife. He stayed there for four weeks, with frequent meetings with the visiting nurses and therapists. On Friday, July 1, we both moved back into our home. I had been away for two months.

By the time six months at home had elapsed, I had *contemplated* what I had experienced and realized that it contributed further to my own evolution—it was a death and rebirth experience. This awareness taught me about *radically letting go* of my bodily and emotional control and turning myself over completely to my inner Wisdom. I actually thought I would die on two separate occasions while in the hospital, but felt no fear. It was a sense that I could "cross-over" quietly and quickly. But almost immediately, in both incidents, I was shown that would not happen.

So I was faced with a need to consent to a long period of healing—the much more difficult road to travel. Great progress has been made in spite of several more medical and physical challenges. I also lost much of my hair and developed an adverse reaction to a blood pressure medication. It took a great deal of will-power and practice to feel secure navigating stairs, and trusting my balance while taking a shower.

A second opportunity that began while I was hospitalized, and continued after homecoming, is the realization of just how kind and caring our five grown children are. Our daughter kept me and her dad in clean clothes for months. One of the demands at rehab was to dress each day as part of the rehabilitation to normal living again. She also grocery shopped for us for several months after our return home, until we were able to do this for ourselves. Our sons visited several times a week and were always on call. The three who live near us frequently advocated for me in situations that arose. Even our daughters-in-law were very kind and helpful.

Our youngest son who lives in Nashville took time to fly up to visit us on three occasions, once with his own eight year old son. Our out-of-town son celebrated his birthday while I was in rehab, and sent me flowers with a note thanking me for giving him birth and teaching him how to be a kind and generous human being. Our children are great examples of caring, caregiving, and partnership.

Medical Patriarchy

My hospital and rehab experience also allowed me a third opportunity, to *observe* how the medical field works. All doctors are not the same, nor all nurses. My primary physician and cardiologist are both highly evolved gentlemen and practitioners. They listen well to their patients and are willing to discuss other topics as well. Both have let me know of their love for me as a person.

Most nurses go about their business (doctor's instructions) with little ability for making alternate choices. It is the gender co-dependent problem for sure. Those who do listen to the patient may become pro-active and seek to influence doctor's orders. One nurse I encountered frequently at rehab, a male, was outstanding at listening to patient distress. He served as an advocate for me on several occasions.

What disturbed me the most was the tendency of nursing staff, regardless of hospital, medical or rehab units, *not to listen* to patients' descriptions of their condition. I witnessed several patients who were ignored and did not advocate for themselves. When I complained about this, and my own condition, to several nurses, I had great difficulty being heard. One case in point was the urinary tract infection I had contracted. It took nearly three days before anyone took action to test a urine sample in spite of my requests. I realized that women in particular are not willing to question the medical staff or complain that something was needed.

In the rehab facility one situation took five days before I convinced the staff that something in my situation needed attention. It was the young male nurse in rehab who heard me, took action and set the matter straight as well as on another occasion. He asked if I would like to speak with a social worker, and I agreed. She listened well and sent the administrative nurse to visit me.

I had three issues I wanted to address, and explained that my concerns had not only been ignored, but that I had also witnessed it with other patients. I also stressed that it was a reflection on their establishment which was excellent on nearly all other factors. The administrative nurse was quite upset and agreed that the matters needed attention and hopefully reform. Even the doctor in charge of the unit came and sincerely apologized to me. Since most of the patients were women, I was once again experiencing the patriarchal gender problem, this time with patients.

When I returned home I realized that enlightened care-giving was available from other nurses and therapists. Those who visited our home treated me not only with respect but with a lot of love. They were nearly all female VNA nurses and therapists who appeared to be freer in their decision making in regard to patients.

Addressing these Issues

We need a genuine *partnership* between doctors and nurses for the sake of the patient. In this way the patient becomes part of the partnership. There is some evidence that there may be a beginning in this direction. My male nurse in rehab, as well as the administrative nurse to whom I spoke, not only admitted the need, but also related some experience with discussions on these matters. At least there is an awareness of this, the first necessary step. Doctors and nurses have complementary functions, not equal, but both equally necessary. There needs to be full discussion of the equality of these functions so that hospital, clinic and rehab nurses are given respect for their service. This is especially true for female nurses because of the gender issues.

I was very fortunate in receiving the care from my cardiologist. He was available at any time, as well as the surgeon he recommended who implanted the pacemaker/defibrillator. Modern medicine certainly can and does work miracles. However, there are serious mistakes made much too often, which will, in all probability, be reversed through appropriate discussion and respect for the very important functions of both doctors and nurses, with a more sensitive focus on the patient. This will be an evolutionary step in the medical field.

Appendices

Appendix A—Gilligan's Research

Gilligan's study involved in-depth interviews with both males and females, matched for age, intelligence, education, occupation, and social class. There were 144 participants, at nine points along the life cycle (8 males and 8 females at each age), beginning at age 6 and up to age 60.[221]

Appendix B—Kegan's Research

Kegan visualized human development emerging in five stages (K-0 through K-5), and as a series of four intermediary structural changes between any two stages. For example, between stages 2 and 3 there are four intermediary positions designated by:

> 2(3) refers to the very small beginnings of a shift,
>
> 2/3 refers to a definite shift but not sufficient to be self perpetuating,
>
> 3/2 refers to a shift which has taken place and is now holding its own momentum,
>
> 3(2) indicates that there is only a residual tendency to return to stage 2 behavior and usually only when one is feeling threatened by past issues.

Stage 2 *behaviors* will never totally disappear; they remain *subsumed* under stage 3 behaviors, as well as any further higher stages attained, because of circumstances which may arise that require such a response. This is true for all stages; they remain but no longer dominate. Altogether there are 21 intermediary phases in Kegan's developmental approach beginning with birth.

Kegan referred to stage 0 as existing from birth until around age two. It is the experience of holding, being taken care of, and merging with the environment. The orientation of stage 1 is entirely toward the immediacy of pleasure, pain, and other sensations. Other persons are seen as *objects* to the emerging self. The ideas, feelings, and wishes of "others" are perceived to be outside of the individual and his/her experience, and are often viewed as oppositional to the developing sense of self.

During the movement from stage 1 to stage 2 the chief focus of the child is on his/her needs, interests, and wishes. If the child conforms to another's wishes, he or she usually feels rewarded, or at least not punished. If there is a lack of agreement or conformity, there is usually a negative reaction on the part of the other and the child feels punished or rejected. Rebellious behaviors are common during this stage and shaming is frequently used for control. A competitive element is noted. With the shift toward stage 3 during adolescence, the tendency is to elicit a growing emphasis on finding ways to please friends and others, particularly among the peer group. Mutuality with one or two close friends becomes desirable. Yet the competitive and achievement orientation remains even though it gradually becomes subsumed into stage 3. At the same time, parents of adolescents often experience opposition from their children. Nevertheless, this is the time when it becomes more and more evident to the developing person that finding others with whom one can agree is a good thing. Agreement with another involves learning how to "take into" one's experience the ideas and feelings of the other and to begin to dialogue mentally with oneself how one thinks and feels about this. There is a sense of making another person's thoughts and feelings one's own to some extent. While this represents developmental progress toward interpersonal relationships (K-3), it also contains the possibility, as well as the likelihood, for forming co-dependent relationships.

The shift from K-3 to K-4 can be quite difficult, due to a tendency to "fall back" into old patterns simply because that is most comfortable. However, unless this tendency is overcome, a person will not be able to understand *self* in terms of personal dynamics, or to distinguish self from others in his/her relationships. The context for the shift to stage 4 usually requires opportunities which offer new interpersonal relationships that shed light on new ways to view the self.

Perhaps a new job or a self-help group can provide this context. Through *reflection* on one's interaction with others, there is an active movement toward preoccupation with self-authorship in both love and work. The person identifies the *self* with the way it is organizing its behavior so as to develop a smoother manner of functioning. The person now perceives the self as the *system,* or manner in which individual uniqueness is now recognized, and in which it is becoming embedded.

There are no easily specified age norms for this transition In the shift beyond stage 4, the person gradually becomes a witness to her unique self, and interested in and available to a kind of sharing or intimacy with others. This is profoundly different from the interpersonal stage 3 in that the new relationships are with other selves as *they* are—individual to individual—and not to one's projections onto them. Now true empathy becomes possible because emotions can be set aside for the sake of knowing the other as other.

The media for this transition toward stage 5 are often religious or political situations, or require relationships that fall outside the usual cultural norm. Reciprocity becomes a matter of simultaneously preserving the other's distinct characteristics while forming a larger context in which separate identities interpenetrate interdependently. No longer will a person tolerate co-dependent relationships that hinder growth, but rather there is a desire to open up to differences so as to share them.

Analysis of movement from stage 0 to stage 2 requires special training in the observation of infant and childhood behaviors. But for analysis of stages 2 and beyond, Kegan's methodology requires discovering what types of situations in the subject's life experience have elicited strong feelings, whether positive or negative. A chart with twelve feeling categories, such as anger/frustration, sadness, joy, forgiveness, is given to the subject who is to be interviewed. The *interviewee* is then asked to note the categories which were outstanding in awareness at that time, and to make notes on the chart concerning the kinds of situations to which they applied. The interviewee then uses this chart for his/her personal use as a reference throughout the interview.

The *interviewer* asks questions only corresponding to the feeling categories which have been elicited by the subject. The purpose for the interviewer is to uncover the underlying "whys" concerning the way in which the subject viewed self and his/her experience. The interviews are audiotaped, transcribed, analyzed, and co-rated with another researcher.[222]

Appendix C—Mid-life Women

My research sample contained equal numbers of early mid-life subjects (age 40 to 54) and later mid-life subjects (55 to 69). I also interviewed a small number of women over 70 in the hope that they might shed light on the shift into the K-4 stage or beyond. Because my research colleague also intended to study mid-life women as well as the relationship between spiritual growth and personal development, we decided to formulate our research methods as a team. She decided to interview women active in various 12-step groups with a focus on the healing process. We reasoned that there would be some commonality between our findings, possibly a considerable amount, that would eventually facilitate a comparison of our samples. It also seemed to be advantageous for us to act as co-raters for each other's data.

My colleague and I had both experienced difficult mid-life transitions, which cautioned us to be careful not to impose our own issues onto the women we interviewed. Therefore, we each initiated a pilot study to insure that the salient issues would emerge uniquely only from the women in our samples. At least two preliminary interviews were conducted by each of us. Only one question was asked, such as "Do you see yourself differently today than when you were young?" or "Tell me about your life." These interviews were audio-taped for one to two hours and then transcribed. In some cases a second interview was conducted to clarify some issues. From the themes that emerged in these preliminary interviews each of us developed a comprehensive questionnaire, pertinent to our individual research focus, which we hoped would be essentially free of our own biases.

Methodology

We designed a multi-method approach: A lengthy, open-ended, *lifespan* interview was constructed from the themes that arose in the pilot interviews, which was meant to gather information not only regarding the *content* of each woman's life experience, but the *context* in which she lived it as well. These lifespan interviews were audio-taped and transcribed, examined for significant themes, and later co-rated for family of origin structure and stability, as well as the degree of parental acceptance and/or rejection, and neglect.

The Myers-Briggs Type Inventory (MBTI)[223], formulated on C. G. Jung's personality theory, was administered to each woman in order to assess individual personality differences, and whether these differences might affect ongoing cognitive development.

The Kegan Subject-Object interview was audio-taped and transcribed. My research colleague and I co-rated both sets of Kegan interviews, frequently with lengthy discussions, in order to come within no more than one intermediary structural change of the other's rating.

This multi-method protocol is known as "triangulation" methodology[224] because it attempts to examine the participants from several *angles* in order to gain a more complete description of the phenomena under study.

Appendix D—Typical Messages

Negative Messages

- "My mother didn't really want me. I wasn't supposed to be here."
- "You nearly killed me when you were born." (Actual words mother to daughter.)
- "Be what I want you to be, maybe even like me. (Mother) But for heaven's sake don't be who you are." "I don't fit in. Where do I fit?"
- "Daddy is dangerous. Do what he says or he might kill me." (Incest) "Get used to abuse, it's normal."
- "Emotional abuse is acceptable even if I don't like it."
- "Keep quiet because I can never be sure that I might say or do the wrong thing. Play it safe."
- "I'm not a good student, I feel stupid."
- "Girls don't need a college education because they will only get married and it will be wasted,"

- "Never get A's because you won't be able to marry if you are too smart."
- "Smart women are a threat to their husbands."

Positive Messages

- "I am a good student; I enjoy succeeding."
- "If I work hard I can accomplish almost anything."
- "Anything worth having is worth waiting for."
- "I can discuss my problems and issues with my parents but make my own decisions."
- "Don't live beyond your means; be content with what you have."
- "Get a good education; it's important."
- "Don't give up on anything."
- "You can, you can, you can—and we will help you."
- "Speak up and you can make a difference."

Messages Capable of Mixed Effects

- "Get married and have the American dream."
- "Don't talk about family matters outside the home."
- "What will the neighbors think? Image is everything."
- "Do what you are told to do, or at least give that impression."
- "It's a mortal sin if you don't go to church on Sunday."

Appendix E—Kegan and Wilber Comparisons

Kegan's Developmental Stages[225]	Wilber's Developmental Stages
K-0 *Incorporative*—embedded in reflexes, sensing, and moving[226]	*Sensoriphysical—sensation and perception*
K-1 *Impulsive*—embedded in: impulse and perception	*Phantasmic-emotional—emotional-sexual, Libido*
K-2 *Imperial*—embedded in: needs, interests, and wished	Representational mind—*symbols and concepts*
K-3 *Interpersonal*—embedded in: mutuality, interpersonal concordance	*Rule/role mind*—can begin to take the role of others
K-4 *Institutional—embedded in: personal autonomy, self-system identity*	*Formal-reflexive mind—self-reflexive and introspective Vision-logic—dialectical and Psychic*—openjng of third eye: lowest of transcendental levels
K-5 *Inter-individual—embedded in: interpenetration of self-systems, integrative*	*Subtle—the seat of archetypes Causal—universal or over-mind*

Notes

1   Brian Swimme, *The Hidden Heart of the Cosmos: Humanity and the New Story,* (Maryknoll, NY: Orbis Books, 1996) p. 3.

2   Patrick Glynn, *God, the Evidence: The Reconciliation of Faith and Reason in a Postsecular World,* (Rocklin, CA: Prima Publ., 1997) p. 26.

3   Glynn, p .23.

4   Tim M. Berra, *Charles Darwin: The Concise Story of an Extraordinary Man,* (Baltimore, MD: The Johns Hopkins University Press, 2009) 15, 29-32.

5   Peter Grant and Rosemary Grant, *How and Why Species Multiply. The radiation of Darwin's Finches.* (Princeton, NJ: Princeton University Press, 2008).

6   John Gribben, *Genesis: The Origens of Man and the Universe.* (New York, NY: Dell Publishing Co., 1981) p. 107.

7   Gribben, p. 187.

8   Gribben, pp. 188-189.

9   Quoted in James Gleick, *Chaos: Making a New Science,* (New York, NY: Viking Penguin Inc., 1987) p. 306.

10 Gleick, p. 307.

11 Wikipedia, *Dinosaurs/Extinction.*

12 Amina Khan, "Fish die-off paved way for evolutionary shift," *The Hartford Courant,* May 17, 2010.

13 Swimme, p.8.

14 Swimme, p.98.

15 Thomas Berry, *The Dream of the Earth,* (San Francisco, CA: Sierra Club Books, 1988) 91.

16 Berry, p. 90.

17 Berry, p. 98.

18 James Lovelock, *Gaia: A New Look at Life on Earth,* (Oxford: Oxford University Press, 1979)

19   Diarmuid O'Murchu, *Reclaiming Spirituality,* (New York, NY: Crossroad Publishing Co., 2000) p. 92.

20   Richard E. Leakey, *The Making of Mankind,* (New York, NY: E. P. Dutton, 1981) pp. 42-43.

21   See also David Pilbeam , quoted in Leaky, p. 52.

22   Wesley. E. Lingren, *Essentials of Chemistry,* (Englewood Cliffs, NJ: Prentice-Hall, 1986) 581-582.

23   Leakey, p. 37.

24   Leakey, p. 29.

25   Stephen Jay Gould, quoted in Leakey, p. 71.

26   Leakey, p. 145.

27   Anne Baring and Jules Cashford, *The Myth of the Goddess: Evolution of an Image,* (London, England: Arkana, Penguin Books, 1991) p. 6.

28   Matt Ridley, "Humans: Why they triumphed", *The Wall Street Journal,* May 22, 2010.

29   Marija Gimbutas, *The Goddesses and Gods of Old Europe, 6500-3500 B. C.: Myths and Cult Images,* (London: Thames and Hudson, 1982); see also *The Language of the Goddess,* (San Francisco, CA: Harper and Row, 1989.)

30   Marija Gimbutas, *The Living Goddesses,* ed. Miriam Robbins Dexter, (Berkeley, CA: University of California Press, 2001)

31   Gimbutas, *The Living Goddesses,* p.xv.

32   Marija Gimbutas, quoted in Thomas Berry, *The Dream of the Earth,* (San Francisco, CA: Sierra Club Books, 1988) p. 144.

33   Thomas Berry, *The Dream of the Earth,* pp. 145-147.

34   Berry, p. 146.

35   Berry, pp. 148-151.

36   Berry, pp. 152-155.

37   Berry, p. 155.

38   Ken Wilber, *Up from Eden: A Transpersonal View of Human Evolution,* (Boulder, CO: Shambhala Publications Inc., 1983) footnote, p. 300.

39   Thomas Berry, *The Dream of the Earth,* (San Francisco, CA: Sierra Club Books, 1988) p. 144.

40   Genesis 3:16, *Jerusalem Bible,* (Garden City, NY: Doubleday and Company, Inc., 1970.)

41 Wilber, p.299.

42 Michael Finkel, "The Hadza", *National Geographic,* Vol. 216 (6), December, 2009, pp. 94–119.

43 Leonard Shlain, *The Alphabet versus the Goddess: The Conflict between Word and Image,* (New York, NY, Penguin/Compass, 1998) p.7.

44 Shlain, pp. 45–47.

45 Shlain, pp. 50–52.

46 Shlain, p. 55.

47 Shlain, p. 7.

48 See Rabbi Rami Shapiro and his discussion in *The Divine Feminine in Biblical Wisdom Literature,* (Woodstock, VT: Skylight Paths Publishing, 2005)

49 Julian Jaynes, *The Origin of Consciousness in the Breakdown of the Bicameral Mind,* (Boston, MA: Houghton Mifflin Co., 1990) p. 4.

50 Wilber, *Up from Eden: A Transpersonal View of Human Evolution,* p. 30.

51 Jaynes, p. 75.

52 Jaynes, p. 93.

53 Jaynes, P. 209.

54 Jaynes, p. 294.

55 Jaynes, pp. 295–296.

56 Rupert Sheldrake, *The Presence of the Past: Morphic Resonance and the Habits of Nature,* (New York, NY: Times Books, 1988) p. xviii.

57 Paul C. W. Davies, *Superforce,* (London: Heinemann, 1984) quoted in Sheldrake, p. 297.

58 Sheldrake, pp. 310–313.

59 Jack Holland, *Misogeny: The World's Oldest Prejudice,* (New York, NY: Carroll and Graf Publ., 2006)

60 Holland , p. 235.

61 Holland, pp. 277–282.

62 Holland, pp. 8–11.

63 Robin Morgan, *The Demon Lover: The Roots of Terrorism,* (New York, NY: Washington Square Press, Pocket Books, 1989)

64 Morgan, p. xvi.

65 Morgan, p. 54.

66 Morgan, p. 18.

67   See Jean Baker Miller and Irene Pierce Stiver, *The Healing Connection: How Women Form Relationships in Therapy and in Life,* (Boston, MA: Beacon Press, 1997)

68   Morgan, pp. 321-325.

69   Allan Guggenbuhl, *The Incredible Fascination of Violence: Dealing with Aggression and Brutality among Children,* tr. Julia Hillman, (Woodstock, CT: Spring Publications, Inc., 1996)

70   Guggenbuhl, pp. 65-77.

71   Morgan, p. 327.

72   Rupert Sheldrake, *The Presence of the Past: Morphic Resonance and the Habits of Nature,* (New York, NY: Times Books, 1988) p. xviii.

73   William Strauss and Neil Howe, *The Fourth Turning: An American Prophecy,* (New York, NY: Broadway Books, 1997)

74   Strauss and Howe, p. 3.

75   Strauss and Howe, p. 6

76   Strauss and Howe, p. 312.

77   Strauss and Howe, pp. 318-320.

78   Bette Friedan, *The Feminine Mystique,* (New York, NY: Norton, 1963)

79   Carol Gilligan. *In a Different Voice: Psychological Theory and Women's Development,* (Cambridge, MA: Harvard Univ. Press, 1982)

80   Robert Kegan. *The Evolving Self: Problem and Process in Human Development,* (Cambridge, MA: Harvard Univ. Press , 1982) See also, *In Over our Heads: The Mental Demands of Modern Life,* (Harvard Univ. Press, 1994).

81   Lawrence Kohlberg. *Collected Papers on Moral Development and Moral Education.* (Cambridge, MA: Center for Moral Education, Harvard Univ. 1976)

82   Nancy Chodorow. "Family Structure and Feminine Personality." In M. Z. Rosaldo and L. Lamphere, eds., *Woman, Culture, and Society.* (Stanford, CA: Stanford Univ. Press, 1974) Also, *The Reproduction of Mothering.* (Berkeley, CA: University of California Press. 1978)

83   Chodorow, quoted in Gilligan, *In a Different Voice,* p. 7

84   Gilligan, p. 42.

85 Carol Gilligan and Lyn Mikel, *Meeting at the Crossroads: Women's Psychology and Girls' Development.* (New York, NY: Ballantine Books, 1993).

86 Deborah Tannen, *You Just Don't Understand: Women and Men in Conversation.* (Ballantine Books, 1990, and Quill Publ., 2001)

87 Gilligan, *In a Different Voice,* p. 62.

88 L. Cahill, "His brain, her brain." *Scientific American,* 292(5): 2005, 40-47.

89 Jaynes, J. (1976, 1990) The origin of consciousness in the breakdown of the bicameral mind. Boston: Houghton Mifflin Co. Also, Shlain, L. (1998) The alphabet versus the goddess: The conflict between word and image. New York: Penguin Books.

90 Erik Erikson, *Childhood and Society,* (New York, NY: Norton, 1963). Also *Identity: Youth and Crisis,* (New York: Norton, 1968)

91 Abraham Maslow, *Motivation and Personality,* (New York, NY: Harper and Row, 1954).

92 Jean Piaget, *The Equilibration of Cognitive Structures,* (Chicago: Univ. of Chicago Press, 1977)

93 Robert Kegan, *The Evolving Self: Problem and Process in Human Development,* (1982), p. 113.

94 This description of Kegan's stages in the following paragraphs has been compiled from Kegan's descriptions in the *Evolving Self.*

95 Judith Jordan, Alexandra Kaplan, Jean Baker Miller, Irene Stiver and Janet Surrey, *Women's Growth in Connection: Writings from the Stone Center.* (New York: Guilford Press, 1991)

96 Robert Kegan, *In Over our Heads: The Mental Demands of Modern Life,* (Harvard Univ. Press, 1994) pp. 266-267.

97 Isabel Briggs Myers and Peter Myers, *Gifts Differing,* (Palo Alto, CA: Consulting Psychologists Press. 1980).

98 Naomi Quenk, *Beside Ourselves: Our Hidden Personality in Everyday Life.* (Palo Alto, CA: Consulting Psychologists Press, CPP Books, 1993)

99 Anthony de Mello, *The Way to Love: The Last Meditations of Anthony de Mello,* (New York: Image Books, Doubleday, 1995) p. 157.

[100] Mary Belenky, Blythe Clinchy, Nancy Goldberger, and Jill Tarule, *Women's Ways of Knowing: The Development of Self, Voice, and Mind,* (New York: Basic Books, Inc, 1986)

[101] Belenky et al, pp. 15-16.

[102] Belenky et al, p. 24.

[103] Belenky et al, pp. 42-43.

[104] Belenky et al, pp. 48-50.

[105] Belenky et al, pp. 93-97

[106] Belenky et al, pp. 101-104

[107] Belenky et al, pp. 133-134.

[108] Belenky et al, p. 138.

[109] Jean Baker Miller and Irene Pierce Stiver, *The Healing Connection: How Women Form Relationships in Therapy and Life.* (Boston, MA: Beacon Press, 1997).

[110] Miller and Stiver, pp. 1-3.

[111] Miller and Stiver, pp.14-17.

[112] Miller and Stiver, pp. 65-66.

[113] Miller and Stiver, p. 81.

[114] Jackson Katz and Sut Jhally, "Tough Guise: Violence, Media, and the Crisis in Masculinity," The Media Education Foundation.

[115] Carol Gilligan and Lyn Mikel, *Meeting at the Crossroads: Women's Psychology and Girls' Development.* (New York, NY: Ballantine Books, 1993).

[116] Jackson Katz, "Men, Masculinities, and Media: Some Introductory Notes," *Research Report,* Vol. 2 (2), Wellesley Center for Women, Wellesley College, MA. pp. 16-17.

[117] Nicholas Kristof and Sheryl WuDunn, *Half the Sky: Turning Oppression into Opportunity for Women Worldwide,* (New York, NY: Alfred A Knopf, 2009).

[118] Kristof and WuDunn, p. xviii.

[119] Kristof and WuDunn, pp. 5-6.

[120] Kristof and WuDunn, pp. 10-11.

[121] Kristof and WuDunn, p. 24.

[122] Kristof and WuDunn, pp. 61-62.

[123] Lucinda Marshall, "The 'Other Terrorism': Militarism and Violence Against Women." *Feminist Peace Network,* in Truthout (http://www.truthout.org), April 16, 2010.

[124] Kelsey Cary, "Combating Human Trafficking in the Western Hemisphere: The Need for Increased NGO involvement." *Council on Hemispheric Affairs,* in Truthout (http://www.truthout.org), July 29, 2010.

[125] Kristof and WuDunn, *Half the Sky,* pp. 17–18.

[126] Kristof and WuDunn, pp. 65–66.

[127] Kristof and WuDunn, pp. 49–53.

[128] Betsy Hood, "Look to Women to End Conflict in Kyrgystan", *Foreign Policy in Focus,* News Analysis in Truthout (http://www.truthout.org), July 13, 2010.

[129] Beverly Bell, "Broadcasting Women's Voices in Haiti's Reconstruction", Truthout (http://www.truthout.org) Op Ed essay, May 4, 2010.

[130] *National Catholic Reporter* (http://ncronline.org) from the series, "Women: Birthing Justice, Birthing Hope". D"mber 1, 2010.

[131] Beverly Bell, "Challenging Globalization Head-on." From the "Women: Birthing justice, Birthing Hope" series in *National Catholic Reporter* (http://ncronline.org) February 23, 2010.

[132] Thomas Fox, "Aiming at Transformation of the World", *National Catholic Reporter* (http://ncronline.org), July 22, 2010

[133] "Religious Women, Empowered and Empowering Others", *National Catholic Reporter,* July 9, 2010. See also Paul Wilkes, "Liberating Nuns of India", same issue.

[134] Angela Bonavoglia, "Women Take on Gender Apartheid in the Catholic Church", Huffington Post (http://www.huffingtonpost.com) August 17, 2010.

[135] Joan Chittister, "Wanted: Women of Spirit in Our Own Time", *National Catholic Reporter* (http://ncronline.org).

[136] "Strength Emerges from the Powerless", essay from *National Catholic Reporter,* May 28, 2010.

[137] Sumru Erkut, "Critical Mass on Corporate Boards: Why Three or More Women Enhance Governance", *Research and Action Report,* Vol. 28 (1), Fall/Winter, 2006, pp. 30–31.

[138] Susan Faludi, *Backlash: The Undeclared War Against American Women,* (Crown Publishing, 1991)

[139] Jackson Katz and Sut Jhally, "Tough Guise: Violence, Media, and the Crisis in Masculinity," The Media Education Foundation.

140 Susan Faludi, *Stiffed: The Betrayal of the American Man*, (New York, NY: Wm. Morrow and Company, Inc., 1999)

141 Faludi, *Stiffed*, pp. 11-12.

142 Faludi, *Stiffed*, pp. 595-597.

143 Faludi, *Stiffed*, p. 583.

144 Faludi, *Stiffed*, p. 599.

145 Betty Friedan, *The Feminine Mystique*, (New York, NY: Norton, 1963)

146 Faludi, *Stiffed*, pp. 600-602.

147 Faludi, *Stiffed*, pp. 603-608.

148 Richard Rohr, OFM, "Sons of Esau: Men in Our Time, Men of Every Time", *Radical Grace*, Albuquerque, NM: Center for Action and Contemplation, Vol. 23 (3), July-September, 2010, p. 3.

149 Randy Markey, "Playing Through Pain", The Jean Baker Miller Training Institute, Wellesley College, Wellesley MA, 2010.

150 Edward Tick, Ph.D., *War and the Soul,* (Wheaton, Illinois: Quest Books, Theosophical Publishing House, 2005).

151 *60 Minutes,* October 17, 2010, CBS.

152 Tick, p. 16.

153 Tick, pp. 17-22.

154 Tick, pp. 4-5.

155 Alexandra Davis, "Many Veterans with PTSD Struggle to Find Supportive Employment," *Los Angeles Times,* September 20, 2010.

156 Tick, pp. 193-197.

157 Tick, pp. 251-252.

158 Nadia Prupis, "Veteran Suicides Outnumber US Military Deaths in Iraq and Afghanistan." *Truthout,* reported October 25, 2010, www.truth-out.org.

159 Kathy Kelly, "War Does This to Your Mind," *Truthout,* reported October 25, 2010, www.truth-out.org.

160 Tick, pp. 28-29

161 Tick, pp. 31-34.

162 Tick, pp.40-43.

163 Ken Wilber, Jack Engler, and Daniel Brown, *Transformations of Consciousness: Conventional and Contemplative Perspectives on Development,* (Boston: Shambhala, 1986) pp.vii-xi.

[164] Carl G. Jung, "Anima and Animus," in *Two Essays on Analytical Psychology,* trans. R. F. C. Hull, (Princeton. NJ: The Collected Works of C. G. Jung, Vol. 7, Bollingen Foundation, Princeton Univ. Press, 1966)

[165] C. G. Jung, "Anima and Animus," paragraph 297.

[166] Emma Jung, *Animus and Anima: Two Essays,* (Dallas, TX: Spring Publications, Inc., 1957, 1985) p.20.

[167] Mary Belenky, Blythe Clinchy, Nancy Goldberger, and Jill Tarule, *Women 's Ways of Knowing: The Development of Self, Voice, and Mind,* (New York: Basic Books, Inc, 1986)

[168] *National Wildlife Federation (NWF),* February/March, 2011, Vol. 49 (2).

[169] Brian Swimme, *The Hidden Heart of the Cosmos: Humanity and the New Story,* (Maryknoll, NY: Orbis Books, 1996)

[170] Rabbi Rami Shapiro, *The Divine Feminine in Biblical Wisdom Literature,* (Woodstock, VT: Skylight Paths Publishing, 2005)

[171] The scriptures passages cited are from *The Jerusalem Bible,* (Garden City, NY: Doubleday and Company, Inc., 1970.)

[172] Diarmuid O'Murchu, *Reclaiming Spirituality,* (New York, NY: The Crossroad Publishing Company, 2000)

[173] O'Murchu, pp. vii–ix.

[174] C. S. Lewis, *The Problem of Pain,* (New York, NY: HarperCollins Publ., HarperOne Books, 2001; orig. MacMillan Publ., 1944.)

[175] St. John of the Cross, *The Dark Night of the Soul.*

[176] Swimme, pp.16-18.

[177] Ken Wilber, *Eye to Eye: The Quest for the New Paradigm,* (Garden City, NY: Anchor Press/Doubleday, 1983) pp. 3-4.

[178] Wilber, p. 271.

[179] Carl Jung, *Psychological Types,* Collected Works, vol. 6, trans. R. F. C. Hull, (Bollingen Series XX, vols. 1-20, Princeton University Press, 1923/1977)

[180] Carl Jung, *Modern Man in Search of a Soul,* (first published in 1933, trans. W. S. Dell and Cary F. Baynes. New York: Harcourt Brace Jovanovich)

[181] Jung, *Modern Man,* pp. 96-97.

[182] Jung, *Modern Man,* p. 100.

[183] Jung, *Modern Man,* p. 108.

[184] Jung, *Modern Man,* pp. 196-198.

[185] Jung, *Modern Man,* pp. 202-205.

[186] Michael Washburn, *The Ego and the Dynamic Ground: A Transpersonal Theory of Human Development,* (Albany, NY: State University of New York Press, 1988) p. 2.

[187] Washburn, p. v.

[188] Washburn, pp. 11-15.

[189] Washburn, pp. 15-19.

[190] Washburn, pp. 10-21.

[191] Washburn, pp. 115-116.

[192] Washburn, p. 146.

[193] Washburn, pp. 153-154.

[194] David Hassel, S. J., *Radical Prayer: Creating a Welcome for God, Ourselves, Other People and the World,* (New York: Paulist Press, 1983).

[195] Hassel, pp. 7-9.

[196] Gerald May, M.D., *The Awakened Heart: Opening Yourself to the Love You Need,* (Harper San Francisco, 1991) p. 52.

[197] Constance Fitzgerald, "The Transformative Influence of Wisdom in John of the Cross", in Joann Wolski Conn, *Women 's Spirituality: Resources for Christian Development* (New York: Paulist Press, 1996) pp. 436-450.

[198] St. John of the Cross, *The Dark Night of the Soul.*

[199] Brother Lawrence, *The Practice of the Presence of God,* trans. Sr. Mary David (New York: Paulist Press, 1978)

[200] May, pp. 142-145.

[201] May, p. 169.

[202] May, p. 191.

[203] May, pp. 195-208.

[204] Robert Kegan and Lisa Lahey, "The Real Reason People Won't Change", *Harvard Business Review,* Product Number 8121.

[205] Robert Kegan, *In over our Heads: The Mental Demands of Modern Life,* (Cambridge, MA: Harvard Univ. Press, 1994)

[206] Andrew Bacevich, "The Unmaking of a Company Man: An Education Begun in the Shadow of the Brandenburg Gate", excerpted from *Washington Rules: America 's Path to Permanent War* (New York: Metropolitan Books, Henry Holt and Co., 2010)

[207] Elizabeth McDaniel, "A Soldier's Homecoming: An Army Psychiatrist Continues His Healing Mission with Today's Veterans, *America,* vol. 203 (13) November 8, 2010.

[208] Edward Tick, Ph.D., *War and the Soul,* (Wheaton, Illinois: Quest Books, Theosophical Publishing House, 2005).

[209] Maureen Dowd, "Worlds without Women", *New York Times,* April 11, 2010.

[210] Riane Eisler, *The Real Wealth of Nations: Creating a Caring Economics,* (San Francisco: Berrett-Koehler Publishers, 2007)

[211] Eisler, p. 214.

[212] David Loye (ed.) *The Great Adventure: Toward a Fully Human Theory of Evolution,* (Albany, NY: State University of New York Press, 2004)

[213] Eisler, p. 215.

[214] Eisler, p. 219.

[215] Eisler, pp. 56-59.

[216] Eisler, pp. 226-227.

[217] Patricia Kraus, "Intergenerational healing: The fruit of personal psychological growth and spiritual transformation", paper presented at the 2000 Theological Symposium on Intergenerational Healing, Toledo, Ohio, Sept. 29—Oct. 1, 2000.

[218] Constance Fitzgerald, "Impasse and Dark Night," in Joann Wolski Conn, *Women's Spirituality: Resources for Christian Development* (New York: Paulist Press, 1996) pp. 410-435.

[219] Fitzgerald, p. 423.

[220] Fitzgerald, p. 424.

[221] Carol Gilligan. *In a Different Voice: Psychological Theory and Women 's Development,* (Cambridge, MA: Harvard Univ. Press, 1982) p. 3.

[222] This description of Kegan's methodology has been compiled from Kegan's descriptions in *The Evolving Self: Problem and Process in Human Development,* (Cambridge, MA: Harvard Univ. Press , 1982)

[223] Isabel Briggs Myers and Peter Myers, *Gifts Differing,* (Palo Alto, CA: Consulting Psychologists Press. 1980).

[224] Patricia Kraus and Barbara Rosen, "The Afternoon of Women's Lives: Triangulation as a Holistic Approach to the Study of Mid-life and Beyond." Paper presented at the 13th International Human Science

Research Conference, St. Joseph College, Hartford, CT., June 14–18, 1994. This paper grew out of our collaboration, especially in our joint rating for both of our samples.

225 Kegan, pp. 118–120.

226 Ken Wilber, "The Spectrum of Development" in *Transformations of Consciousness: Conventional and Contemplative Perspectives on Development*, (Boston: Shambhala, 1986) pp. 69–74.

Bibliography

Bacevich, Andrew. "The Unmaking of a Company Man: An Education Begun in the Shadow of the Brandenburg Gate", excerpted from *Washington Rules: America's Path to Permanent War* (New York: Metropolitan Books, Henry Holt and Co., 2010)

Baring, Anne and Jules Cashford, *The Myth of the Goddess: Evolution of an Image,* (London, England: Arkana, Penguin Books, 1991)

Belenky, Mary, Blythe Clinchy, Nancy Goldberger, and Jill Tarule, *Women's Ways of Knowing: The Development of Self, Voice, and Mind,* (New York: Basic Books, Inc, 1986)

Bell, Beverly. "Challenging Globalization Head-on." From the "Women: Birthing justice, Birthing Hope" series in *National Catholic Reporter* (http://ncronline.org) February 23, 2010.

_____"Broadcasting Women's Voices in Haiti's Reconstruction", Truthout (http://www.truthout.org) Op Ed essay, May 4, 2010.

Berra, Tim M. *Charles Darwin: The Concise Story of an Extraordinary Man,* (Baltimore, MD: The Johns Hopkins University Press, 2009)

Berry, Thomas. *The Dream of the Earth,* (San Francisco, CA: Sierra Club Books, 1988)

Bonavoglia, Angela. "Women Take on Gender Apartheid in the Catholic Church", Huffington Post (http://www.huffingtonpost.com) August 17, 2010.

Cary, Kelsey. "Combating Human Trafficking in the Western Hemisphere: The Need for Increased NGO involvement." *Council on Hemispheric Affairs,* in Truthout (http://www.truthout.org), July 29, 2010.

L. Cahill, L. "His brain, her brain." *Scientific American,* 292(5): 2005, 40-47.

Chittister, Joan. "Wanted: Women of Spirit in Our Own Time", *National Catholic Reporter* (http://ncronline.org).

Chodorow, Nancy. "Family Structure and Feminine Personality." In M. Z. Rosaldo and L. Lamphere, eds., *Woman, Culture, and Society.* (Stanford, CA: Stanford Univ. Press, 1974)

_____*The Reproduction of Mothering.* (Berkeley, CA: University of California Press. 1978)

Davies, Paul C. W. *Superforce,* (London: Heinemann, 1984) quoted in Sheldrake, p. 297.

Davis, Alexandra. "Many Veterans with PTSD Struggle to Find Supportive Employment," *Los Angeles Times,* September 20, 2010.

de Mello, Anthony. *The Way to Love: The Last Meditations of Anthony de Mello,* (New York: Image Books, Doubleday, 1995)

Dowd, Maureen. "Worlds without Women", *New York Times,* April 11, 2010.

Eisler, Riane. *The Real Wealth of Nations: Creating a Caring Economics,* (San Francisco: Berrett-Koehler Publishers, 2007)

Erkut, Sumru. "Critical Mass on Corporate Boards: Why Three or More Women Enhance Governance", *Research and Action Report,* Vol. 28 (1), Fall/Winter, 2006, Stone Center, Wellesley College, Wellesley, MA.

Erikson, Erik. *Childhood and Society,* (New York, NY: Norton, 1963).

_____*Identity: Youth and Crisis,* (New York: Norton, 1968)

Faludi, Susan, *Backlash: The Undeclared War Against American Women,* (Crown Publishing, 1991)

_____*Stiffed: The Betrayal of the American Man,* (New York, NY: Wm. Morrow and Company, Inc., 1999)

Finkel, Michael. "The Hadza", *National Geographic,* Vol. 216 (6), December, 2009, pp. 94-119.

Fitzgerald, Constance. "Impasse and Dark Night," in Joann Wolski Conn, *Women's Spirituality: Resources for Christian Development* (New York: Paulist Press, 1996) pp. 410-435.

_____"The Transformative Influence of Wisdom in John of the Cross", in Joann Wolski Conn, *Women's Spirituality: Resources for Christian Development* (New York: Paulist Press, 1996) pp. 436-450.

Friedan, Bette. *The Feminine Mystique,* (New York, NY: Norton, 1963)

Fox, Thomas "Aiming at Transformation of the World", *National Catholic Reporter* (http://ncronline.org), July 22, 2010.

_____"Religious Women, Empowered and Empowering Others", *National Catholic Reporter* (http://ncronline.org, July 9, 2010. See also Paul Wilkes, "Liberating Nuns of India", same issue.

Gilligan, Carol. *In a Different Voice: Psychological Theory and Women's Development,* (Cambridge, MA: Harvard Univ. Press, 1982)

Gilligan, Carol and Lyn Mikel, *Meeting at the Crossroads: Women's Psychology and Girls' Development.* (New York, NY: Ballantine Books, 1993).

Gimbutas, Marija. *The Goddesses and Gods of Old Europe, 6500-3500 B. C. : Myths and Cult Images,* (London: Thames and Hudson, 1982)

_____*The Language of the Goddess,* (San Francisco, CA: Harper and Row, 1989.)

_____*The Living Goddesses,* ed. Miriam Robbins Dexter, (Berkeley, CA: University of California Press, 2001)

Gleick, James. *Chaos: Making a New Science,* (New York, NY: Viking Penguin Inc., 1987)

Glynn, Patrick. *God, the Evidence: The Reconciliation of Faith and Reason in a Postsecular World,* (Rocklin, CA: Prima Publ., 1997) p. 26.

Grant, Peter and Rosemary Grant, *How and Why Species Multiply. The radiation of Darwin's Finches.* (Princeton, NJ: Princeton University Press, 2008).

Gribben, John. *Genesis: The Origens of Man and the Universe.* (New York, NY: Dell Publishing Co., 1981)

Guggenbuhl, Allan. *The Incredible Fascination of Violence: Dealing with Aggression and Brutality among Children,* tr. Julia Hillman, (Woodstock, CT: Spring Publications, Inc., 1996)

Hassel, David S. J. *Radical Prayer: Creating a Welcome for God, Ourselves, Other People and the World,* (New York: Paulist Press, 1983).

Holland, Jack. *Misogeny: The World's Oldest Prejudice,* (New York, NY: Carroll and Graf Publ., 2006)

Hood, Betsy. "Look to Women to End Conflict in Kyrgystan", *Foreign Policy in Focus,* News Analysis in Truthout (http://www.truthout.org), July 13, 2010.

Jaynes, Julian. *The Origin of Consciousness in the Breakdown of the Bicameral Mind,* (Boston, MA: Houghton Mifflin Co., 1990)

Jordan, Judith, Alexandra Kaplan, Jean Baker Miller, Irene Stiver and Janet Surrey, *Women's Growth in Connection: Writings from the Stone Center.* (New York: Guilford Press, 1991)

Jung, C. G. *Modern Man in Search of a Soul,* (first published in 1933, trans. W. S. Dell and Cary F. Baynes. New York: Harcourt Brace Jovanovich)

_____ "Anima and Animus," in *Two Essays on Analytical Psychology,* trans. R. F. C. Hull, (Princeton. NJ: The Collected Works of C. G. Jung, Vol. 7, Bollingen Foundation, Princeton Univ. Press, 1966)

_____ *Psychological Types,* Collected Works, vol. 6, trans. R. F. C. Hull, (Bollingen Series XX, vols. 1-20, Princeton University Press, 1923/1977)

Jung, Emma. *Animus and Anima: Two Essays,* (Dallas, TX: Spring Publications, Inc., 1957, 1985) p. 20.

Katz, Jackson and Sut Jhally, "Tough Guise: Violence, Media, and the Crisis in Masculinity," Video from the Media Education Foundation.

Katz, Jackson, "Men, Masculinities, and Media: Some Introductory Notes," *Research Report,* Vol. 2 (2), Wellesley Center for Women, Wellesley College, MA. pp. 16-17.

Kegan, Robert. *The Evolving Self: Problem and Process in Human Development,* (Cambridge, MA: Harvard Univ. Press , 1982) See also, *In Over our Heads: The Mental Demands of Modern Life,* (Harvard Univ. Press, 1994).

_____ *In Over our Heads: The Mental Demands of Modern Life,* (Harvard Univ. Press, 1994)

Kegan, Robert and Lisa Lahey, "The Real Reason People Won't Change", *Harvard Business Review,* Product Number 8121.

Khan, Amina. "Fish die-off paved way for evolutionary shift," *The Hartford Courant,*

May 17, 2010.

Kelly, Kathy. "War Does This to Your Mind," *Truthout* (http://www.truthout.org), reported October 25, 2010.

Kohlberg, Lawrence. *Collected Papers on Moral Development and Moral Education.* (Cambridge, MA: Center for Moral Education, Harvard Univ. 1976)

Kraus, Patricia. "Intergenerational healing: The fruit of personal psychological growth and spiritual transformation", paper presented at the 2000 Theological Symposium on Intergenerational Healing, Toledo, Ohio, Sept. 29—Oct. 1, 2000.

Kraus, Patricia and Barbara Rosen, "The Afternoon of Women's Lives: Triangulation as a Holistic Approach to the Study of Mid-life and Beyond." Paper presented at the 13th International Human Science Research Conference, St. Joseph College, Hartford, CT., June 14-18, 1994. This paper grew out of our collaboration, especially in our joint rating for both of our samples.

Kristof, Nicholas and Sheryl WuDunn, *Half the Sky: Turning Oppression into Opportunity for Women Worldwide,* (New York, NY: Alfred A Knopf, 2009).

Lawrence, Brother. *The Practice of the Presence of God,* trans. Sr. Mary David (New York: Paulist Press, 1978)

Leakey, Richard E. *The Making of Mankind,* (New York, NY: E. P. Dutton, 1981) Lingren, Wesley E. *Essentials of Chemistry,* (Englewood Cliffs, NJ: Prentice-Hall, 1986) 581-582.

Lewis, C. S. *The Problem of Pain,* (New York, NY: HarperCollins Publ., HarperOne Books, 2001; orig. MacMillan Publ., 1944.)

Lovelock, James. *Gaia: A New Look at Life on Earth,* (Oxford University Press, 1979)

Loye, David (ed.) *The Great Adventure: Toward a Fully Human Theory of Evolution,* (Albany, NY: State University of New York Press, 2004)

Markey, Randy. "Playing Through Pain", The Jean Baker Miller Training Institute, Wellesley College, Wellesley MA, 2010.

Marshall, Lucinda. "The 'Other Terrorism': Militarism and Violence Against Women." *Feminist Peace Network,* in Truthout (http://www.truthout.org), April 16, 2010.

Maslow, Abraham. *Motivation and Personality,* (New York, NY: Harper and Row, 1954).

May, Gerald M.D. *The Awakened Heart: Opening Yourself to the Love You Need,* (Harper San Francisco, 1991) p. 52.

McDaniel, Elizabeth. "A Soldier's Homecoming: An Army Psychiatrist Continues His Healing Mission with Today's Veterans, *America,* vol. 203 (13) November 8, 2010.

Miller, Jean Baker and Irene Pierce Stiver, *The Healing Connection: How Women Form Relationships in Therapy and in Life,* (Boston, MA: Beacon Press, 1997)

Morgan, Robin. *The Demon Lover: The Roots of Terrorism,* (New York, NY: Washington Square Press, Pocket Books, 1989)

Myers, Isabel Briggs and Peter Myers, *Gifts Differing,* (Palo Alto, CA: Consulting Psychologists Press. 1980).

National Catholic Reporter (http://ncronline.org) "Strength Emerges from the Powerless", essay from May 28, 2010.

National Catholic Reporter (http://ncronline.org) from the series, "Women: Birthing Justice, Birthing Hope". December 1, 2010.

National Wildlife Federation (NWF), February/March, 2011, Vol. 49 (2).

O'Murchu, Diarmuid. *Reclaiming Spirituality,* (New York, NY: Crossroad Publishing Co., 2000)

Piaget, Jean. *The Equilibration of Cognitive Structures,* (Chicago: Univ. of Chicago Press, 1977)

Prupis, Nadia. "Veteran Suicides Outnumber US Military Deaths in Iraq and Afghanistan." *Truthout,* reported October 25, 2010, (http://www.truthout.org)

Quenk, Naomi. *Beside Ourselves: Our Hidden Personality in Everyday Life.* (Palo Alto, CA: Consulting Psychologists Press, CPP Books, 1993)

Ridley, Matt. "Humans: Why they triumphed", *The Wall Street Journal,* May 22, 2010.

Rohr, OFM, Richard. "Sons of Esau: Men in Our Time, Men of Every Time", *Radical Grace,* Albuquerque, NM: Center for Action and Contemplation, Vol. 23 (3), July–September, 2010.

Scriptures passages cited are all from *The Jerusalem Bible,* (Garden City, NY: Doubleday and Company, Inc., 1970.)

Shapiro, Rabbi Rami. *The Divine Feminine in Biblical Wisdom Literature,* (Woodstock, VT: Skylight Paths Publishing, 2005)

Sheldrake, Rupert. *The Presence of the Past: Morphic Resonance and the Habits of Nature,* (New York, NY: Times Books, 1988)

Shlain, Leonard. *The Alphabet versus the Goddess: The Conflict between Word and Image,* (New York, NY, Penguin/Compass, 1998)

St. John of the Cross, *The Dark Night of the Soul.*

Strauss, William and Neil Howe, *The Fourth Turning: An American Prophecy,* (New York, NY: Broadway Books, 1997)

Swimme, Brian. *The Hidden Heart of the Cosmos: Humanity and the New Story,* (Maryknoll, NY: Orbis Books, 1996)

Tannen, Deborah. *You Just Don't Understand:Women and Men in Conversation.* (Ballantine Books, 1990, and Quill Publ., 2001)

Tick, Edward, Ph.D. *War and the Soul,* (Wheaton, Illinois: Quest Books, Theosophical Publishing House, 2005).

Washburn, Michael. *The Ego and the Dynamic Ground: A Transpersonal Theory of Human Development,* (Albany, NY: State University of New York Press, 1988) p. 2.

Wilber, Ken. *Up from Eden: A Transpersonal View of Human Evolution,* (Boulder, CO: Shambhala Publications Inc., 1983)

_____*Eye to Eye:The Quest for the New Paradigm,* (Garden City, NY: Anchor Press/Doubleday, 1983)

_____"The Spectrum of Development" in *Transformations of Consciousness: Conventional and Contemplative Perspectives on Development,* (Boston: Shambhala, 1986

Wilber, Ken, Jack Engler, and Daniel Brown, *Transformations of Consciousness: Conventional and Contemplative Perspectives on Development,* (Boston: Shambhala, 1986)

Wikipedia, *Dinosaurs/Extinction.*

CPSIA information can be obtained at www.ICGtesting.com
Printed in the USA
LVOW10s1955071016

507864LV00015B/961/P